The Offbeat

The Offbeat:

I Have Been Sometimes True To Nothing

A Literary Collection

Edited by Theresa Mlinarcik

Michigan State University Press - East Lansing

The paper used in this publication meets the minimum requirements of ANSI/NISO z39.48-1992 (1997) (permanence of paper)

Library of Congress Cataloging-in-Publication Data

The offbeat : I have been sometimes true to nothing : a literary collection / edited by Theresa Mlinarcik.
    p. cm.
ISBN 0-87013-678-X (pbk. : alk. paper)
1. American literature--Michigan. 2. Michigan--Literary collections.
I. Mlinarcik, Theresa, 1980-
PS571.M50356 2003
810.8'09774'090511--dc21
2003008601

Cover and Interior Design by Julia Nicole Herzog

Michigan State University Press
East Lansing, Michigan 48823-5245
http://www.msupress.msu.edu
Printed and Bound in the United States of America

Contents

Her Laugh Was a Line Drawn Firmly

Defenestration

Her Laugh Was a Line Drawn Firmly

Spring
Josh Guilford

winter weather withered.
depth of dawn delivered.
a yellow yawn,
the sunrise song:
"beginnings for beginners."

The Way to Life
John Garcia

I always wondered why they called it "Indian Summer"

the end of September
a time not close enough to be Summer
      but yet, too far away to be called Autumn
            (despite the red and yellow of the leaves)
a time of endings that is also a time of beginnings

a time where nature shrouds her canvas with
    morning mist and chill of fog
       revealing it under an afternoon sky bright with promise
         only to shroud it again under a dark new moon
    changing and revealing a new work under a new sun of life
                 save for harvest moonlight
                 when, for a brief moment of sight
                 you can watch the drops of dew
                 sparkle and shine as they paint
                 the leaves in colors new and old
                 they, the tears of the artist
                 who must again destroy his creation
                 for the sake of itself
            for from life, is the truest art revealed
            this living canvas, born of time and word
            new in each sight and life
            framed for viewing by a day like today
            to inspire a being like this
                held in stasis
                     and joined in time

a time where life walks the paths of crunchy leaves in bare
feet
       crinkling and crackling like a fire
          a fire that burns not in the woods, but in the heart
              the flame of the heart
the flame that shows the life where the path leads

how it's okay to run and jump into the just-raked
leaves
only to rake them up and jump into them again
the flame that shares the secrets of the dying leaves
showing them written on the stems and vines of each one
nature's parchment, ready to be mounted and framed
(revealing a different secret to everyone)
quiet poet, quiet your mind
and listen to my last song
blowing through the empty branches
as I mourn my children
how fast they grow
only to die
salt of the earth
now only grains of sand
mourn them poet
mourn them as I do
and then you will know
holding one in my hand, I feel its crinkle and hear its crunch
then, my hand closes
the pieces fall out, and I brush them away
remembering that there are always remnants
when life ends
pieces that never really leave
but become one with the wind
I envy those pieces
for they are going where my soul longs to be
beyond the horizon
and around the corner
from the next sunset

evergreen

a time where love waits to be found
beyond passionate promises and soulful soliloquies
to a place where a hand holds more than another hand
and where a glance whispers more than orators
could ever speak
precious days fade too quickly like the early sunset

preparing us not to face the too long night alone
through his picture window, he can see them
　　he can see the currents of his time blow away the
　　　　　leaves of his memories from the trees of his life
　　red and yellow, it is time for them to be cleared away
　　　　　to be replaced by new leaves, new memories
save the ones that will remain despite the wind, despite the
winter of forget
　　　　　leaves that will remain ever-red
　　　　　　　　(pieces of his heart)
　　that will always be among the inner leaves
waiting the Spring

　　　　　　　　　now my poet
　　　　　　　　　see me come through
　　　　　　　　　in slatted streams
　　　　　　　　　of twilight waters?
　　　　　　　　　hear me come over
　　　　　　　　　in colored pages
　　　　　　　　　of daylight novels?
　　　　　　　　　all I await is you
　　　　　　　　　the time has come poet
　　　　　　　　　　to mourn
　　　　　　　to let go of the Indian Summer
　　　　　　　　　of youth
　　　　　　　and to embrace the Autumn
　　　　　　　　　of years
　　　　　because Summers are always short
a Spring that remains too far away
　　too far away from life
　　　　too close to death
the song decays off of the foliaged ceiling
　　and comes down as rain
　　　　from the new gray overhang
we line up to gather our heathered robes and our candles
　　taking our place, ready to enter the darker days
　　　　when time moves slower
　　we hood ourselves as the chant begins
　　　　　　wordless, a song of Gaia
　　　　　　　and everything changes

I always wondered why they called it "Indian Summer"
        but now,
                I know

it is a death
        on the way
                to life

The Story of Lugau

Jeremy Couillard

Dear Sirs,
      *On a summer's day, while exploring around the
woods where I live, I came across a giant clearing. I had
walked through that forest many times, and never had I seen
such a clearing. It was around the size of an athletic stadi-
um. While walking around the area a bit, I started to notice
pieces of wood sticking out from the ground. They were no
larger than a step; with symbols written all over them in
faded black ink or some were carved into the wood. I began
picking up one after another, and soon, I noticed that I could
place some together as if the pieces of wood were parts of a
giant jigsaw puzzle. Placing a few pieces of wood together,
the symbols on them looked something like this:*

      *I spent all day in the mysterious clearing. In past
walks I dreamed of finding such things. I was never actively
searching them out, but I had always wished for something
to make my lonely life more exciting in its last years. I
placed together many wooden steps, all with strange symbols on them, that intrigued me more and more as I discovered that the symbols could be writing, and the writing could
tell of an ancient civilization not yet known to the western
world. When night came, I covered steps in leaves and
marked my path so that I could return.*
      *In the weeks that followed I became obsessed with my
discovery. I had to decipher the symbols; I had to discover
the history of the clearing in the woods. Being a poor old
widower with no living family or friends, I decided to take
up the research myself. For months I consulted libraries
across the Midwest, but to no avail.*
      *I was about to use my life savings to travel to Europe
to visit the Bibliothéque Nationale when one night, just on*

chance, while walking through a gigantic university library, ready to renounce my search, a peculiar book caught my attention: on its binding were faded symbols that looked very similar to those from the site in the woods. Immediately I pulled the book out from the shelf and began looking through it. Le Lugau et sa langue, it was called. The French author did not give his name. I opened the book and the symbols were clearer. They were those that I needed to decipher. From excitement and a feeling of strange coincidence that I should have found such a book, a rush of energy surged through my body and I nearly fainted. In the book, it told of an ancient American civilization that came from Asia thousands of years ago. There is very little evidence of their existence, but the author claims that he became good acquaintances with the last Lugau (for that was their name) on earth. From this old, blind man, the author learned the language and customs of the people. His book included a comprehensive study of the very language I needed to translate. Since the acquisition of this book, nearly two years ago, I have studied its symbols intently, so much that I can read the writings on the pieces of wood with little effort. I have read all that I have found and have completed the history for myself. For the others, I fear that the translation to English was not easy. I only managed to translate three stories.

I'm afraid, gentlemen, that I haven't the energy to continue in my old age. I can feel that my last days are near. I submit to you in this packet: my three humble translations, the book of Lugau culture and language, and map of the said site. (in terms of translation, I am no professional. Some Lugaun terms such as sp-anraq, I have translated to the western lute. Sp-ung keepo, I have translated to coliseum. Although the tower in Lugau was most likely not very much like a Roman coliseum, and the sp-anraq was most likely a bit different from a lute. I have made notes throughout my translation that may clear up some confusion). I hope that you find this information not only fascinating but also useful. Please do not look for me. By the time you receive this I shall be dead.
All best wishes,

Luis Penelope
October 24th

I. Entertainer of the Dead

My grandfather was an entertainer of the dead, my father was an entertainer of the dead so, naturally, I also chose this profession. Their instrument was the lute, and they passed their skill and knowledge down to me. Who am I to change this tradition? When I die, just like all others, I want my body to be carried to the coliseum and there I will be entertained until the day when God comes to take us to his eternal paradise.

I must confess, through, that it is a rather dreary profession. Everyday I must make the long walk to the coliseum outside the city gates. Everyday I must sit in its center, looking out at the hundreds of thousands of dead bodies, the flies, the decay. And there I am, right in the middle of everything, a tiny little speck strumming a lute and humming songs, looking out and wondering if anyone is listening. I light a giant hanging incense burner that sways back and forth above me, spreading its smoke. This helps keep the smell out, but sometimes when there is a war or famine and numerous fresh dead bodies are brought in, the smell makes me vomit. I would guess that my vomiting is more entertaining for the dead than my lute playing. I don't have a very large repertoire: maybe just a few hundred short songs. I play almost the same thing every eight-hour shift. I am an old man now, and my mind doesn't learn like it use to when my father would teach me songs.

Sometimes I wish we thought differently. I wish that we thought like some of the other tribes who came here to trade: that when a man dies, his body belongs in the ground and his soul goes someplace else, a place more pleasant than earth. I ask these artisans, how could a soul leave the body? Where would it go? To this they have vague responses that are no better than mine. I can never be sure of any answers to my questions. We, the Lugau, are certain that the soul stays that person's senses. The very thought of the soul leaving the body scares me. What if I did? We would surely know. We would be able to see it, hear it or feel it. We could never prove what happens to the soul, so we must assume that it stays in its body, and with it its senses of sigh, smell, vision and hearing; all waiting for their creator to take them back to their origin. I never understood how the artisans who come through my village could make the leap of faith that when they die, their soul leaves. I imagine the terror of being buried in the ground while you stare into darkness, feeling worms eating your flesh. This fear alone causes most of us to follow in the ways of our ancestors. When a man dies, his body stops working and that is all. Families do not grieve. They simply take their relative to the coliseum where he will wait for his creator. They come to visit their relative and bring him flowers, little trinkets, or sometimes will attempt, to no avail, to engage the relative in a game of chess or some other diversion. They may cry because there is no longer any communication between them and the relative, but they know that they will soon join this person when the time comes.

People who question such a process are sometimes lynched and then buried in the ground. We cannot have heretics. These traitors are buried in a cemetery deep in he woods where they are forgotten forever. Even though the though of this ever happening to me sends chills of fear up and down my spine, I, like many, have questioned our practices. I am still alive simply because I kept my thoughts secret.

I was a young man when I started my career entertaining the dead. My wife came with me to dance while I played my lute. In those days, I was very ambitious. I liked my job. I liked that I was important to many people, that I kept them entertained. Everyday after work I would practice the lute with my father and learn new songs, scales, and chords. Sometimes I even wrote my own childish songs, which I still occasionally play to this day:

The Lugau are a fabulous race
If you don't believe me, I'll cut your face

Then returning home with my wife, we would eat a large meal together, make love and sleep well.

As time passed, though, my sleep became disturbed by questions I could not answer. "What if God never does come down to the coliseum to collect the dead as the prophets tell? Is there a God? A soul? Why do our people believe differently than everyone else?" But the thing that concerned me the most was, if there was neither a soul nor a God, then I was spending all my days entertaining no one. My career and life were meaningless.

My wife and I began whispering to each other during dinner. She also had been thinking such thoughts since she was a child. But who were we to question the ways of our ancestors? We did not want to join the cemetery of heretics. But the thought of being buried in the ground for an eternity was just as bad as the thought of being useless. We decided that when there were no more priests or guards in the coliseum, we would do some experiments with the dead. We both had never known a dead person before and weren't sure how to begin. For lack of any other ways to prove that the dead were listening to us, while I played my lute, my wife began dancing among the bodies in the stands and singing songs quietly in their ears.

Can you hear me can you see me?
Does my dancing give you glee?
What happens after death, please tell me.

She danced around the dead all day whispering such things to the tune of my lute. When she was done she walked down from the stands and stood next to me. I didn't feel anything. We turned around in circles, looking at the bodies. Some were skeletons, some were brown with decay and some were fresh with smells so pungent that they could almost be seen floating around them. But not one gave us any sign that they acknowledged us, that they wanted us to continue entertaining them: no thunder, rain, or even the slightest movement.

When my wife and I went home that night we weren't hungry and we couldn't make love. We could no longer blissfully accept the dogma of our forefathers, but in the same way, we still could not completely reject it. "Maybe they will give us a sign later," my wife suggested. We waited for years, testing the dead in new ways, and every year that passed our faith in our ancestors and culture diminished. As time went by we became recluse, old and confused.

After the death of my wife five years ago, I have been making the journey to the coliseum alone. The lute strapped over my shoulder is my only companion. I sit in the middle of the coliseum and I look out at the decay; my wife's body blends among the multitude, barely recognizable besides the flowers I bring to her every week resting on her lap. Does she hear the songs I play to her? Do her companions in death want me to go on? I will never know. My whole life has been a waste and now soon I will be dead. I have no family or friends. A government worker will wheel me out to the coliseum and place my limp body on the stands. Will I be conscious? Who will play the lute for me? Who will entertain the dead when I am gone?

II. Manifesto For the People of Lugau Posted on Coliseum Entrance

Our ancestors told us to preserve the bodies of the dead. They told us that God would come for them. They said that if we put them in the ground God couldn't take their souls. We placed all of the dead in a coliseum. We have been expanding on the coliseum for hundreds of years and now we cannot expand any longer. It is too massive. We can now see its walls from our village, and on a windy day the stench blows into our homes. We can no longer wait for God, so we must find him. Our ancestors said many generations ago that God lives in the clouds and that when he comes to get us, that is also where we will go. We cannot wait, though. We will begin our ascent into the clouds to find God and make Him realize we are here.

People of Lugau, I urge you to begin building toward the heavens! If we continue entertaining the dead, they will use up all of our resources, and soon our village will be a ghost town. Take your hammer, take your wood and begin building stairs up toward God. This is our last chance before we all join our ancestors in the coliseum waiting for Someone who will never come for us!

III. The City of Stairs

We were a forgotten city. God didn't know who we were, or perhaps He was dead, decaying up in the heavens that not even we could reach, with no one to entertain Him. After the revolution, we stopped working in pursuit of God. Everyone stopped everything in order to build a staircase high enough to reach the heavens. We began in the coliseum of the dead because that was the highest building in our village. We ripped wood from the coliseum and let the dead fall to the ground. Many people during this time began to question the old ways of our people. They did not believe that when we died, our souls were trapped in our bodies. At first, some were lynched but eventually people stopped caring. Everyone believed that there was something up in the sky and exploring that was more important than adhering to the ancient ways of our elders. For our whole lives we looked up at the sky and at the clouds and wondered what the celestial objets held. When the revolution came, it gave the whole village a chance to find God in their own way.

The first staircases constructed intertwined with each other. The village's two richest men built them in cooperation, in such a way so that when one man was going up his staircase, the other couldn't see him. This way they could sneak in extra work when the other wasn't looking and they could get to God first. These two staircases did not last long due to the men's poor building skills and clumsiness. Both men fell from the tops of their constructions and died. With the two superpowers dead, the people of Lugau felt that they could now begin their personal ascensions into heaven without the rich men's assailants harassing them. Other staircases were attached to these two and then others were attached to those that were attached to the originals...and so on, and so on.

By this time, the entire coliseum of the dead lay in shambles. Dead bodies covered the ground and jutting up from the pile of death rose the stairways. The whole town had been converted into a maze of stairs.

The building became more and more obsessive everyday. So much to the point that now, most people live in the sky and no longer return to the crumbling village. The only time anyone goes close to the ground is to get wood, which the woodcutters supply (the woodcutters being some of the only people known to live on the ground). Rainwater is collected to quench our thirst. And for our hunger, some have started small gardens on platforms they made in their staircase, and others have resorted to cannibalism. We are so obsessed with finding God that we have resorted to eating each other in order to not have to take the time to descend to the earth for food. Every person is alone in his small hut, hiding in his own little corner with a knife to fend off attackers, only leaving a night to secretly build a few steps higher.

I now sit in my small shelter I have built to protect myself. There are two small windows. One is to see if there are attackers coming and the other has a view of clouds. We are high in the sky now and from my window the beautiful formations made by clouds in the morning are the only pleasure I have. Also in my hut are gardening tools, a pile of wood, and writing instruments with which I write my story. In the early morning I take wood from my pile and work on my staircase, which expands from the roof of my small home. While I build I look out among the vast web of other staircases. Sometimes I see other people but we are all so scared of each other. I, like many others, have lost most of my motivation to keep building. I build around five steps a week. We take our knives and attempt to carve our history because we know that it is taking its last breaths. I often wonder, while I build or write in my stairs, if we were better off before, with the coliseum of the dead and the belief of our ancestors.

In the end of the book, Le Lougau et sa langue, *the author tells of the collapse of the giant staircase. There was a war between two small stair tribes. Someone of the two burnt down a section of one tribe's staircase; not realizing his was connected to the one he burnt, that all staircases were somehow connected. This caused the entire structure to collapse. Several people survived, but were so agonized by the fall of their society that they could not start over again and died among the rubble. Building stairs was all they knew. The ways of their ancestors had been nearly lost: just a few sto-*

ries remained written on the stairs. One old man did survive, though, took a sack and some food and set out through the forest. The forest traveler met with the mysterious French author and it is because of the meeting of these two men that the book on Lugau language and culture was written and I was able to decipher the language written on the steps and learn of their history.

Locked Corners
Suzanne Spiegoski

Bright necks decided on purple after patches of skinny grip
Tire marks in lavenders of innocence
The dark echoes befriend you in the cold corner,
Waiting feels war to the blind floor-
For he hides beneath your feet - somewhat a comfort.
Rough palms collide and time becomes wasteful days
Realize the anguish in your own truth
a squared room is the only reason your mind moves,
and hands dryer than your mouth.
It must be the blocked wall screaming,
You're wanted as much as the weeps carried on.
Who wants to blame the lost illusions you're facing?
Hands run off onto the wall with permanent scars.
I'm sure it's missed especially in the afternoon,
Where you sip your soup and wrap a hot towel around your
head.
That's what it must be, what else is there to live by?
Hoping for it, no... there is no such way!
Forgiveness is where I throw your dreams
with my dirty basket of clothes.

Private Manifesto
Julia Herzog

a moment of you,
and I'm forever porcelain.
you arrive on time,
to remind me of all that's lost
with dark haunting eyes

a confirming presence
takes command of my motions
without an uttered word

I'm shattered in a ritual of interaction
hello, goodbye,
and those phrases behind you

learning to keep face,
to be the one you forget
the irony locked in mouth
now I remain perched
upon the corners of dishonesty

as if I were a tropic bird
lost in perpetual loop
between the longitudes
of a Siberian land

frozen since the hour I lied
created my private asylum
awaiting this manifesto
written for him, to him

waiting in an ethereal confessional
for a man that will never arrive
on the other side of these words

Ink on Paper
Gregory Wright

The woman undressed, frozen in a pose. She looked over her shoulder coyly, licking her lips. She seductively pulled at her garters.

"Who the hell wears garters these days, anyway?" she asked.

Not knowing and not caring, Stuart shrugged his shoulders. The woman's hips jutted to her left, probably further than was comfortable, and her nipple peeked out of her lingerie. She pouted her lip with practiced precision in a look that, while sexy, reminded Stuart of his younger cousin. He banished the thought, sliding his hand down his pants.

"Ooh, big boy," she said with a sly smirk, "you know what turns me on."

Stuart didn't care what turned her on, his hand kept working.

"Yeah, that's right. Worthless, self-absorbed men in nowhere jobs get me hot ... And, oh yes, oh yes, do that, do that. Masturbate right there. Ejaculate in less than five minutes. I *love* chubby, insecure guys who don't think twice about what I might want."

He looked very closely into her eyes to see if she had really just said that, or if he'd just imagined it. Her eyes couldn't tell him much. Just two blurry inkblots of light transferred onto paper by an impersonal printer. Little dots spattered across the page.

Stuart wiped off the dirty magazine, and hopped into the shower. He was late for work. He put on his shirt and knotted his noose of a necktie, saving his pants for later.

He adjusted his tie as his boss approached. Stuart rearranged his desk to look organized, forgetting that he'd put things there to clutter the otherwise blank space. Stiffening his back, he stared at the screen as if he were concentrating ... or going blind.

"Hey, Sam," his boss said, "How's the accounting spreadsheet going?"

Stuart didn't have the heart or the spine to correct his boss. For the past two years, Stuart had maintained the company web page, and Stuart's name was Stuart, not Sam. Stuart answered with a kind of circular nod that could have been a yes or a no. The boss moved on without waiting for a response anyway, clicking his pen as he went. "You know why the pen is mightier than the sword?" the boss asked no-one-in-particular in his biweekly stale joke. "Because the pen signs the checks!" Stuart heard his boss was a millionaire on paper. Whatever that meant. Stuart figured his boss could afford a joke writer. "Get it? The pen signs the checks!" Stuart didn't know how to react.

Stuart unzipped his pants and let fly with a lengthy jet of urine and a thunderous fart. He wished there were some graffiti to entertain him. He splashed pee on the white porcelain of the urinal. He'd write some graffiti on the wall himself if he weren't secretly afraid that the company'd installed video cameras in the light fixtures. It was irrational, but then, it was an irrational company. In a fleeting act of rebellion, he spontaneously gave the light fixtures the finger, and immediately feared that someone had seen him. Of course they'd recognize him; he was a bathroom regular. Typically, he could time things just right so that he never did much work. When he came back to his cubicle, he'd sit down and settle in ... when, whoops, he'd need another drink from the water cooler. Stuart needed to consume an excessive amount of water to continue his bathroom break trickery. If anybody ever asked him why he went to the bathroom so often, he'd thought up the excuse that he was fighting a bladder infection. Nobody ever asked him, though.

Stuart had not set out to be a professional bladder master. When young Stuart was asked about his future, he never said "I want to be a mindless cog in a faceless company, doing thankless tasks for endless hours." He hated designing web pages as much as he hated the company he did it for. Oddly enough, he wasn't any good at making web pages, and his efforts didn't represent the company very favorably. If anyone noticed, though, they didn't discuss it with him.

They showed him pictures of lungs blackened with

cancer. They told him smoking was gross. He agreed. Yet Stuart was considering taking it up because it could afford him excuses for more breaks. If he did start smoking, he'd definitely roll his own cigarettes, so his break would take even longer while he fiddled with getting the tobacco on the paper.

After washing his hands and ruining some paper towel, Stuart performed a quick pit check. Sniff ... sniff ... the right was okay, but the left was a little rank. Stuart sniffed it again, enjoying the manly stink of his left armpit. Only a true stud could work up such a stench. The temporary feeling of virility brought his focus back to his crotch, and he remembered to zip his fly back up.

"What, you mean you already put that whole big thing away?" asked Evie, the attractive young accountant behind him.

Stuart didn't respond, but his face turned very red. He set the empty water glass, which he'd drained far too quickly for normal human consumption, back down on his desk. Someone had finally caught him in his water-drinking scheme! And it was the pretty accountant in the cubicle behind his. The star of his bathroom breaks' masturbation fantasies – she was actually talking to *him*!

"You thirsty or what?" Evie leaned over his cubicle wall, her breasts pushing up against the edge. Stuart immediately looked away for fear of being caught staring. In passing glances, he loved to look at her skin, which was so pale it was almost translucent. Stuart imagined he could see her veins through her skin as a seductive road map to all her erogenous zones. He turned his head and cleared his throat as if he had work to get back to. Evie slipped back down on the other side. Stuart silently congratulated himself on his clever tactical maneuvering to avoid discussion of his water-and-urine work avoidance cycle. His blank computer screen had an air of mockery Stuart didn't like. To destroy the scornful white space, Stuart typed "Holy Toledo!" onto the screen four and a half times. He deleted it before someone walked by and saw that he wasn't working.

So then Jesus signed at the dotted line with a flourish of his pen and they all became roommates: Jesus,

Mohammed, and Buddha. That was the premise for the sit-com Stuart wanted to write, "Holy Toledo!" Stuart knew it was brilliant, having often read the unwritten reviews in his mind: "a wacky show about three single guys with nothing in common who share an apartment in Toledo." "Screwball comedy!" "Delightful fun!" Being roommates, they'd have funny little spats; they'd threaten to "nail Jesus' ass to the wall," and other sacrilegious gags. Stuart had two episodes on paper, and ten more floating in his head. The idea of a script fascinated Stuart; it was paper that created a world and commanded its people. It was perfectly self-contained.

"Why the hell am I reading this? Is it *supposed* to be funny?" Stuart's parents, on the other hand, thought he ought to have a back-up plan, "in case that whole Mohammed thing doesn't pan out." His father wrote him an e-mail: "Why don't you go into something with computers? Making a web page can't be too different from writing the stuff you like to write. They're both creative. Whatever you do, though, you know that your mother and I support you." Stuart snickered when he read that, because he knew he'd be financially cut off if he didn't do what his father wrote. No more little portraits of presidents in green ink. Just like when the report card came home with bad grades printed on it. He knew how his father was. Stuart could read between the lines.

So Stuart worked on web pages. The words he typed became a kind of electronic script. He controlled and shaped a world, but it was a far, far duller world than those zany bachelors' apartment. The computer monitor's photons of light created the illusion of putting ink on paper, though nobody in reality nobody would ever print it. If anyone ever even looked at it. He sighed and reluctantly laid his hands on the keyboard.

Stuart quickly licked his fingers so he wouldn't drip anymore and stain his pants. He wiped up the pizza sauce with a blank white napkin, regretting his request for the waitress to write "extra sauce" on her order tablet. He needed to hurry if he didn't want to be late for work. He always had the back-up excuse of having car trouble if anyone asked why he was late, even though he walked everyday to the same restaurant. Nobody ever asked him, though. He hoped the waitress would refill his root beer again so he could pee when he got back to work.

An ass came down on his foot. Stuart nearly choked when he saw whose it was. Evie's. His foot was touching her ass! Not quite the sensual encounter of his fantasies.

"Oh, excuse me," she laughed, "Do you mind if I sit here?"

Stuart took his foot off the other chair at his table, and Evie sat down. So much for a relaxing lunch alone. She looked at the menu for what seemed like forever. He was definitely going to be late if he was expected to wait for her. Stuart looked at his watch.

It was steaming and covered with onions. Paper thin, chalk white onions. And it took ten minutes! Stuart knew because he'd looked at his watch. He was going to be late, she was going to have bad breath, and now this stinky, onion-covered pizza was being thrust at him.

"Want some?" Evie asked. The cheese threatened to singe his offended nose. He shook his head. While waiting for her food, Evie told him her background and goals. Stuart kept nodding and sneaking peeks at her chest. For being so attractive, though, Evie was disgusting when she ate, like a cow chewing a pulpy wad of cud. Stuart tried to ignore it by staring at the images on the restaurant's yellow wallpaper.

Stuart saw thirteen men sitting on one side of an enormous table. He decided he'd sit on the other side of the table, figuring that these were important people who he didn't want to mingle with, lest he lose his anonymity. Evie sat next to him, and grabbed the notebook she always brought to company meetings to record the minutes. For a second, Stuart mused that recording minutes is the exact opposite of writing a script; one mirrors the world, the other creates. He didn't think about this long, though, as he noticed that pizza sauce had dribbled down the front of his new white shirt in a perverse, vertical Morse code. He tried to hide the stain. The meeting began. Looking left, he realized Evie, too, had spilled some sauce, making her white shirt look like a Japanese flag. He pointed at it, and she blushed two Japanese flags onto her cheeks. Stuart looked into her eyes, trying to convey how bad he felt for her. She smiled back slightly.

The topic of loss was discussed. Graphs showed how performance didn't match previous graphs. Stuart's boss droned on and on, an impressive lecture for not having notes. After this monologue of loss, an efficiency expert was introduced. Stuart's stomach knotted in fear of the corporate headhunter. Visions danced in Stuart's head of a lie detector with this burly efficiency expert, the needle scribbling wildly across the paper while Stuart spoke of his bathroom breaks. Dark circles began to seep onto Stuart's shirt under his arms. He did not feel like a stud.

The muscle-bound superhero held his right hand in a fist as he flew, stoically setting his jaw in grim determination against the forces of evil. Stuart vaguely recognized the superhuman personality from a comic book. Stuart wondered if this was the same superhero who always had his strength-increasing war hammer with him. He couldn't tell since the character's left hand was below his superhero waist, obscured by the edge of the sleeve. The efficiency expert had rolled his cliché sleeves up to show he meant business, but exposing his action figure tattoo somewhat undermined the effect. Something other than terror popped into Stuart's mind.

"Fat!" The expert paused, his eyes darting to see who was sweating. "Yes, that's right, fat! That's the problem with this company! Someone needs to trim the fat! The budget's horrible, projects take forever, and we pay corpses, for God's sake! Corpses!" Nervous snicker. "You laugh, but payroll actually sends checks to a dead man because his time sheets still get filled out! We need to stop this! We need to trim the fat!"

His fat jiggled as he stood up. His white cotton shirt made his gut look like a giant blob of correctional fluid. "He's absolutely right," piped in Stuart's boss. "Anybody here remember Stuart Plume?" Stuart was about to speak up, when his boss kept going, "We all miss him. He did some great work for us, but now he's gone."

Niagara Falls. Tidal waves. Floods washing away whole towns. Stuart couldn't understand it. Why was he being singled out? It made him very nervous, and being nervous made him need to pee. All the fluids he'd been drinking didn't help, either. What kind of sick game was his boss playing?

"Russian roulette, apparently," continued Stuart's boss, "Stuart Plume played a solitaire game of Russian roulette, if you will, and lost. The police said the apartment's carpet was dyed red with blood. He killed himself several months ago, but someone keeps writing out his time sheet. We're going to get to the bottom of this, too. A major company overhaul is underway."

"Hey! That's a lie, Stuart's right here," boomed Evie, pointing. Stuart would've joined in, but he was busy having a panic attack. His eyes bugged out, his tie felt too tight. Stuart slumped in his chair, paralyzed. "He isn't dead. We had lunch together today! He's not dead!"

"What? You mean Sam?" asked Stuart's boss, "No, I'm talking about Stuart the web page writer, not Sam the accountant."

"I know him. This *is* Stuart Plume!" she cried, "I know him. He isn't dead!"

One of the fat executives felt Evie up. He'd been holding her shoulders for ten minutes, taking deep breaths along with her to calm her down, and then he slyly groped her as he backed away. "There, there," he kept saying, the final *there* being her left breast. Evie was too shocked by other circumstances to register the executive's harassment. Stuart had long ago flopped to the floor and lay there ignored. Nobody in particular had the ulterior motive to feel him up.

Stuart was dead. Stone cold dead. That's what his file said. No matter what he said to them, it had all the necessary paperwork, often in triplicate. Death certificate. Funeral service information. Copies of the condolence letters sent to his parents. Etc. Stuart couldn't think of anything official that proved his existence. He had no counter-evidence. The only thing legal was his signature, and that could easily be a forgery.

He figured he'd start filling out his time sheets under the name "Sam" now. Just because he was dead didn't mean he should stop making a living. If he did things right, maybe nobody would notice.

When Smiling Dogs See in Threes
Nicole Bernadette Birkett

it's midnight on a Wednesday in march,

the weather smacked an old injury,
sent me into a small coma,
and brought me to a dull throbbing,

and all I want is a drink.

ex-lover number one sits at my bar,
sporting a white T-shirt and new girlfriend,
a shiver inspiring ensemble.

I'd really like that drink,

but the bar is almost empty,
there's a premature last call,
and my one beer is carried by ex-something number two,

also wearing a T-shirt,

and though green,
I can still see where shoulder rubs shoulder
before sliding into neck,

a cruel line.

I find it difficult to finish my beer,
too distracted by seams,
and I fail to notice number three

giving me the come-hither-and-converse tilt.

I saw one,
and tossed out a nod of recognition,

I saw number two,
and grimaced,

but when three walked in

I grinned like a dog.

Popular Poetry Royalty
Crystal Passmore

ramble and rant and scream me a lullaby, dear prince
fuck my ears with your popular poetry
because i bow not to your words
and works
and rules of syntax
but dance on dotted vowels,
swim in dictionary dreams,
and put question marks
at the end
of declarative sentences.
you are a fountainhead fuehrer
furious because
my words slam into walls
and slip off the roof of my mouth
like sleepless insanity
then take off running
before rhyming
with love or lust or death
in my own vain attempt
to be warp-speed beat poetry
with hyphens and periods
and pauses that defy
punctuation
as I masturbate with alliteration
and say
fuck off, your royal majesty

The Mexican Tuxedo

D. Harlan Wilson

I was daydreaming about movie stars and martini bars when
a sentient Mexican tuxedo crept up behind me and attached
itself to my body. My daydream dissolved like a pinch of salt
that's been sprinkled into a glass of water. All of a sudden the
real world was staring at me, and I was caked in denim from
neck to ankle.

Jeans and a jean jacket now encased my body. Not only that,
the jeans were too tight, and the jean jacket buttoned itself up
all the way to my neck.

I tried to take the Mexican tuxedo off, but it wouldn't let me.
And the harder I tried, the firmer its grip became on my flesh.

"Yesterday a man told me that my ear holes had hair in
them," I said to the man standing on my left without looking
at him. "And now this shit. When it rains it pours, I guess.
Life's like a child—cruel as hell."

Keeping his head still, the man carefully glanced at me out of
his eye corners. He was naked. So were all of the other men
who were standing on the edge of the cliff.

I had been naked once. I wished I was again.

I screamed.

The man who was looking at me out of his eye corners
winced. He told me to pipe down and stop making a spectacle
of myself. "We're trying to step off this cliff in a dignified,
gentlemanly fashion," he said. "You're making that difficult to
do." A few other men confirmed this sentiment with garish
nods of approval. I asked them all how they would feel if
what happened to me happened to them. They responded

with facial expressions that indicated a complete lack of empathy in their emotional make-ups.

I screamed again, louder this time. A shockwave rippled across the Mexican tuxedo's stiff, dark blue skin. The portion of its skin encasing my crotch tightened up, warning me not to do that again.

I listened to its warning.

Another naked man inched up to the edge of the cliff. He cracked his knuckles, slicked back his eyebrows with a pinky finger, rearranged his lips, nodded . . . and casually stepped off. It was long way down. Infinitely long. At the bottom of the cliff was a bottomless abyss. The man would not die in the next minute or two from striking the ground at 800 mph. He would die in the next few days from lack of food and water as his body, along with the bodies of the men that had preceded him, continued to fall into nothingness.

The sky above us was a rich pastel violet that seemed to have been painted there.

The abyss below us was the color of my soul.

The Mexican tuxedo was itching me. I told it to stop. It didn't listen to me.

Hoping to wound the outfit, I threw myself on the ground as hard as I could. The outfit didn't get hurt. I did.

Another man stepped off the cliff and nosedove into infinity. Not a peep came out of his mouth as he shrunk to the size of a pinprick...

Men were stepping off the cliff in no particular order, but only one man was allowed to step off at a time, and before the next man stepped off, the man that stepped off before him had to disappear from sight. This took about thirty seconds. So far, about fifty men had stepped off the cliff. Including me, there were about one million men left.

It was our duty to do what we were doing. We had nobody to answer to and there were no consequences if we decided to stay put. It was simply our duty. And everybody was doing it.

I didn't want to do my duty with the Mexican tuxedo on. A man should fall to his death in his birthday suit, not in clothes, certainly not in clothes that violated normative standards of fashion and had racial connotations. Not to mention that the clothes I had on—or rather, the clothes that had put themselves on me—were alive.

Granted, it was a little flattering that the Mexican tuxedo had chosen to attach itself to me out of everybody else. I felt special, even though I was being tyrannized. But I felt more annoyed and embarrassed than special. Some men started to smirk and snigger. Others went so far as to make belittling comments about my character.

I ignored my oppressors until one of them tapped me on the shoulder. In a pragmatic tone of voice, he said, "You lack good taste, sir. I have a right mind to slap you across the face. In fact, I believe I will slap you."

He slapped me. He was a scrawny, balding thing with limbs like dead tree branches, unlike my limbs, which, when they were exposed, exhibited various and sundry muscular bulges and a webwork of imposing purple veins. The man had used all of his strength when he slapped me, but the slap did nothing more than send my head to one side and produce a wincing expression on my face. If I were to have slapped the man back with all of my strength, I may have broken his neck, or at least sent him airborne. I would have liked to do that. But the Mexican tuxedo wouldn't let me slap him back; the arms of the jean jacket stiffened up on my arms and concretized them at my sides. I could only fix my eyes on the man and say, "You are a bastard, my friend. A bastard, and a fucking asshole. It's obvious that I'm in no position to retaliate against you. Does irritating people who lack the means to irritate you back make you happy?"

The man slapped me again. Before he had used the back of his hand. This time he used his palm, and the noise that echoed into the distance was the noise that results from two bare-assed clams smacking into each other at high speed.

The Mexican tuxedo shuddered with glee. I think I might have even heard it giggle.

Wrath welled up in me like hot lava rushing up the cone of a volcano on the brink of eruption, but I had no means whatsoever of acting upon that wrath. The Mexican tuxedo was my master, and I was its slave. The outfit had also rendered me the slave of the man who was beating me: he could do anything he wanted to me and I had no choice but to endure it. What had I done to deserve this domination? If only I could take a few steps forward and put an end to it.

Despite the circumstances, however, I was not about to let weakness get my goat. I titled up my chin, widened my eyes and nostrils, and shouted, "I know who I am! Whatever you do to me, it won't change anything! I'll still be the same man I've always been!" The exclamation was not only for the man who had slapped me, but for the Mexican tuxedo and every last cliff-dweller, too.

I was answered by a communal outburst of laughter that only diminished as more men continued to step off the cliff and fade away. And before each man stepped off the cliff, he made a point of passing by me and leaving his mark on my face.

My face was slapped roughly one million times. Sometimes forehands were used, sometimes backhands. Sometimes the slaps hurt, sometimes they didn't. Sometimes I bled and cursed, sometimes I didn't bleed and kept my mouth shut.

Sometimes I wanted to die, sometimes I wanted to use a flamethrower to annihilate everything that is, was and ever will be alive...

The only way I managed to stay on my feet while undergoing slap after slap was because the Mexican tuxedo had gone rigid as the bark of a petrified tree. I was frozen in the position of a soldier at attention. After a while my neck became rubber and my head teetered back and forth like a meatball on a clock spring. But my body stood tall.

When the last man had dropped out of sight, the Mexican tuxedo's skin slackened and slipped off of me. Barely conscious, I collapsed. My face was a black, bleeding, swelled-up bruise, and I lacked the strength to get up and step off the cliff, let alone crawl off it.

My head bore the handprints of humanity. I could feel the handprints throbbing and squirming like so many livewire eels...

Before I passed out, I lifted my head up off of the cold dirt of the cliff. Squinting through blood and tears, I watched the Mexican tuxedo salute me, do a quirky little dance, and finally swan dive, gracefully, into an empire that I would never have the pleasure of knowing...

The Rodent Speaks
Theresa Mlinarcik

"Now that I have lost you
I cannot allow you to develop,
you must be a photograph not a poem."
-Jeanette Winterson

I speak of you in only past tense.
I speak of you like I retell my nightmares to strangers.
I speak of you with a sigh in my voice.
I speak of you as if you are a dead rodent that lives behind the furnace.

I've written about you for years. I've been published for you, to prove to you I could write. That I could do something with words. That I could do something you couldn't.
I was hoping you'd find the words scattered around the city and look at them. That you would bump into them accidentally. But you would never go looking for words. Never find them on your own.

I scribble notes about you and forget I've written them. I write long tired pages in the dim. I type words while I hum them aloud.

I begin to wonder if I write while I'm sleeping. I wake up with a pen in my hand, ink on my breasts. I wake up because the room is heavy with stillness, with only the sound of my uneven breathing.

I'd like to think of our time apart as a separate being.
A character in a play I performed many years ago, while I was still an amateur, still in Acting 101.
"I can't remember much about him, except that he had less lines than anyone else."
This character (now only a mention in my portfolio of work)

would be aging gracefully, would have taken his bows and exited.

But instead it has only been a short time.

I would like to know it has been a significant amount of time since I finally stopped missing you.
I'd like to say it has been 7 years since I once loved you.
16 years of not thinking of you.
That it happened sometime in my youth. "It was a silly time, really."
"Goodness, I can barely remember what his face looks like nowadays. We were both dreadfully young, you know."

Some kind of phrase that turns time into words, into a substantial block of space. Into a flip-book of pictures. Into an overplayed song. Maybe a former favorite novel, but now I'm older and appreciate those who break the rules of narrative.

You are still awake somewhere in this house. I can smell a day when we cooked something fragrant. I can see a shadow cast on the wall of your figure.

The rodent behind the furnace calls your name. And he remembers everything, everything.

Disconnect
Carl Armstrong

You and I are as intimate as phone sex,
connected only through faceless, cigarette-smoking phone
operators.
Through the electric synapse that pulses in inconsistent
bursts,
our misguided interaction begins as a rough and clumsy
dance.
Your confused rhythm pounds through my body,
incoherent as a scream, indecisive as the wind,
and I'm lost. I can hear your breath in my ear
and feel your hands crawling slowly up my skin,
discarding cells like drunken inhibitions.
My body is your airport,
and my mind is the distraught passengers who run
in hopes of making flights,
just to watch that last plane sail into the stratosphere.
You are my phantom limb,
coming and going at your own convenience.
Despite this, addicted, I call again.
Again, no one answers.

Vodka
Amanda Goodrich-Stuart

You've been with
your soul mate
again
tonight.
I can smell her
on your
breath.
She makes you
love me
more.
For all the
wrong
reasons.

But you never
were
very good
at it on your
own.
You always needed
her help.
I almost like you
better when
she holds your
hand
in the
dark.

That Woman
Crystal Passmore

That woman's

as pure as frost white
skin stretched over a smiling
face,

as happy as rose s-
tained cheeks tainted
red with life

(and Mabelline),

as soft as spring flowers
clutched
in her cold hands like
crucifixes
clutched in a dead corpse-

gray coffin to match the green grass
of her dress,

she's
as ceremonial as formal-
dehyde,

and more loved than the impression
of a well attended funeral,

as alive as the taut smiles, and nice-
ly formed tears
and memories
wrinkling/wrinkling/wrinkling.

They Beat Me Near Death, But The Pay Is Good

Richard Lund

She told me to pick her up at eight thirty. I've been sitting in my car a block away from her apartment since seven. I didn't really have anything else to do, so I figured it would be better to show up early. Now it is eight twenty-five, and my palms are sweating like crazy. My hair isn't as nice as when I left the house, and my ass itches a bit from sitting here so long. I'll have to remember not to show up so early next time.

I get out of my car, and everything is in slow motion. By the time I have walked up the four stairs of her porch, I'm almost blacking out. I can barely ring the doorbell. She comes to the door and invites me in. She isn't quite ready yet, she tells me. That is what my dad always said about girls; that they are never ready on time. She leaves me in the living room so that she can finish up getting ready. "She's putting on her face," is what dad would have said. Just when she is out of sight, I notice a cockroach fall out of my pant leg. It hits the floor and makes a dash for under the couch. My dad always said that after the big war comes, that the roaches will be the only things left on earth. She comes back into the living room and is ready to go.

As we drive to the movie theater, I try to think of something captivating to say. No such luck. I don't think I've ever said anything captivating. I don't even think I really know what the word means. I've never been that smart. All I really know tonight is that I think the girl next to me is beautiful. I might not know what captivating really means, but I know that she's it. She is all the definition of the word I need. I want to do something that will make her think about me what I think about her. I want to do something for her. Help her. That's what dad said women want. Someone to help them. We talk about the weather until we get there.

I park the car and get out. I walk around to her door. Dad said to always be a gentleman when with a lady. I reach for the handle to open it, and a scorpion falls out of my sleeve.

I look at it, while it stands on the pavement, pinching at my shoe. It is looking back at me, straight into my eyes. I kick it under the car and open the door. I grab her hand and help her out. This earns me a smile. I grab her hand as we walk up to the front doors. She holds it. Another roach falls out of my sleeve, but it isn't the hand that is holding hers. Lucky, for both of us.

I buy our tickets from a young man in his twenties. He looks at me as if he knows what I am and what kind of farce I'm trying to pull. He doesn't say anything, though. We walk into the theater and sit down. The movie starts. We are still holding hands. Occasionally, I can see out of the corner of my eye her looking at me. It is almost a motherly look. She must be seeing the tribe of ants that are crawling out of my collar, up the back of my neck. They don't really bother me that much. I can almost pretend that they are not there. The movie is about a family that falls apart. It is a drama, I think. My dad always said that women like dramas. He said that dramas were girl movies, and that if I ever had a wife I'd see my share before my time was up.

The character who is the mother of the family in the movie passed away. I felt like I identified with her a little bit. It is quite sad. I feel what I at first think to be a beetle crawl down my face, but when I go to brush it away, I realize it is a tear. My date sees this, and she must think it is captivating because she puts her arm around me. How strange. She kisses my cheek, and I feel something. Something different than what I'm used to. Something dad never described to me. A python slides out of my pant leg, onto the floor, and down the aisle.

After the movie, we drive home. She rests her head on my shoulder as we pass the miles by. Gnats fly out of my hair and into the wind the whole way home. We pull up to her house and I walk her to her front door. It doesn't seem like the same place it was four hours ago. She asks me if I would like to come inside, but I told her that I shouldn't. Dad always said that you shouldn't spend too much time with any woman until you know them well. She says that she is sorry to hear that. She moves towards me, and I can feel the gears inside me quicken. She comes closer with her head and her mouth moves next to mine. I can feel a rat in my mouth, clawing and scratching, trying to jump out. I hold it back with my tongue the best that I can. She kisses me. The rat is gnawing on the back of my throat, wanting out, as I gently kiss her back. She finishes it, and smiles at me. Into her house she retires. I quickly turn my head and spit the rodent out.

I run around her house to her back yard and climb over the fence. I go behind some bushes and find some soft dirt underneath her bedroom window. I claw at the earth and dig a hole. I do this as fast as possible, and when I'm finished, my hands are bleeding. I think I really like this girl. Wasps are beginning to exit from my mouth and ears. I crawl into the hole and cover myself with leaves and grass. I won't come out until next Friday when the two of us will be going out to eat. Night comes, and I can't really tell if I'm decomposing, or if I'm turning into decomposers. Captivating.

Farming Woes
Chris Bigelow

A landless man is no man, we believe
Of corn and hay we own manifold fields
Upon our homes the agencies aggrieve
From growing suburbs' progress we have reeled
By droughts or floods or banks we've had to go
But seldom do those terminate our farms
Who cares that from here comes the world's bread dough
They all desire the simple country charm
Where bovines amble acreage closed with barbs
Where husbandry of beast compares to man's
Where boots and overalls denote the garb
Where aged farmers don't have pension plans
Bucolics pioneered this land of ours
The milk and honey void of them goes sour

Fluff an' Taffeta

Nicole Bernadette Birkett

I remember when my uncle started raisin' rabbits. He thought the world was gonna end when all the computers crashed, an', 'cause he hadn't really started payin' attention to the news 'til late October, an' he had only like a month an' a half to get ready, I guess he thought rabbits were his best bet.

Me and the rest of the kids on the block thought it was a great idea. Not that there weren't a lotta animals around, you couldn't walk more'n twenty feet without bein' attacked by a different cat, or hounded by someone's Doberman, but it was kinda like a neighborhood project. Our school was just a couple a'blocks away, so afterwards us kids would stop by his house, peek over the fence, an' see how far we could chuck outta the yard who's ever cat was creepin' towards the bunnies. 'Sides, bunnies is real sweet, too bad my aunt didn't see 'em that way. Aunt 'Mandla was so ashamed of those rabbits an' more ashamed of her husband.

She really didn't have that much to be ashamed of; farm animals aren't unheard of in the city. Actually, guy next door to me and my ma has chickens in his backyard, an' the old lady two doors down from my aunt an' uncle used to have two guard geese, 'til one of the Dobies got loose an' ate one. Now the lady just has one goose, meaner than shit, hoppin' around on one leg. Nah, Aunt 'Mandla just didn't like nothin' common an' rabbits are almost as common as her husband. If them rabbits had worked at the factory with my uncle and the rest of the neighborhood, I'm sure Aunt 'Mandla would've been equally ashamed of 'em both.

My ma and my aunt 'Mandla were always thinkin' that they deserved better men, men outside of the neighborhood, richer men. Her an' my ma were always braggin' 'bout some "wealthy relations in the South." I'm not sure where "in the South" these "relations" were, but they must of been pretty far South, 'cause every year it took my ma and aunt 'Mandla two weeks to get back from what was s'pose to be a one week visit. They always left on the first Saturday of November, so I was stayin' with my uncle when he got the rabbits, an' I was still stayin' with him when Aunt 'Mandla came home with my ma.

Aunt 'Mandla took one look at me lying on the couch with that oversized cotton-ball on my chest an' started to scream at my uncle, "William, is that an animal in my house?"

Uncle Will just kinda smiled, an' put his hand on the back of his head, "Nothin' ta be frightened of 'Mandla, just a lil'l boy."

I started to laugh, an' the rabbit jumped offa me and hopped over to Aunt 'Mandla, an' she just stared at it like it'd just asked her for a quickie out back.

My ma gave me a come-here-or-else look, an' I got up and thought that maybe it'd be better if I came back to get my things later.

"Come on with me son, *we* are going home." Then Ma turned to Aunt 'Mandla, "I will see *you* later Amandla." And she just 'bout spit at Uncle Will with her eyes before she shoved me outta the door.

~~~~~~

I didn't really get to visit 'em too much, what with school, an' my uncle workin' all the time, an' I didn't wanna visit the rabbits with just Aunt 'Mandla 'round. But, when our Christmas break started, an' Ma went to live with her boyfriend for a while, I got ta stay with Uncle Will, an' Aunt 'Mandla, an' the rabbits.

I was never quite sure what it was exactly my uncle said to Aunt 'Mandla to let him keep the rabbits, but Uncle Will always made sure to keep 'em outta her sight when she was around.

While I stayed at their place I slept on the couch in the livin' room, an', 'cause the heater broke, Uncle Will snuck in one of the big bunnies to sleep with me. He said that the bunny, with his lil'l heart beatin' so fast, would keep me plenty warm, I just had to make sure that I, "...put 'em back in the shed 'fore Aunt 'Mandla wakes up. An' if he starts ta get antsy, take him into the bathroom and set him on the litter box in the corner."

I didn't know how Uncle Will planned on hidin' a litter box from Aunt 'Mandla, 'specially in the only bathroom in the house. I told Uncle Will that Aunt 'Mandla was sure to be real mad in the mornin'.

"Nah, your aunt an' I've worked it out. Don't worry. As long as the animals are offa the furniture an' outta her sight, an' not makin' any messes, ya can have 'em inside. So ya better hide 'em under the blankets tonight."

When I did wake up the next mornin', it was 'cause I heard someone bein' awfully loud in the kitchen behind me. Aunt 'Mandla was cursin' the toast that I guess she'd burned, though I didn't smell anything burnin'. The rabbit had climbed out of the blankets an' was sittin' on top of my chest, sniffin' my face. I grabbed him fast an' tucked him under my nightshirt. When aunt 'Mandla turned her back to dump the toast in the garbage, I hurried out the door.

The snow made my bare feet numb an' when I came back into the kitchen Aunt 'Mandla was bent over the stove.

"What were you doing outside in your pajamas? Get into that bathroom and wash your feet in some warm water...and use the bathtub! And watch that you don't stain your cloths with that sink spraying rusty water."

I was hurrin' away from her 'fore she started askin' too many questions, when she yelled,

"Make sure you give your blankets a shake before you fold them. *Then* you come back in here for your breakfast."

~~~~~~

Uncle Will seemed awfully happy when he came home from work that night. He'd snuck up behind Aunt 'Mandla an' grabbed her 'round the waist, an', while givin' her a big hug, put somethin' in her hand.

"What are these?"

"They're tickets ta the Mayor's New Year's Ball. My foreman couldn't go, 'cause his wife's real sick, but he knows how much you're always likin' ta get out to movies and fancy places."

I think Aunt 'Mandla almost smiled 'fore she pushed

Uncle Will off her.

"We can't go."

"Well, why not 'Mandla?"

"You have nothing decent to wear and I don't have anything nearly nice enough."

Uncle Will turned an' looked at me, like he was askin' me what he should do. I didn't know how I should be lookin' back, but I must of done somethin' right, 'cause Uncle Will got this big grin on his mouth, an' he rested his chin on his thumb, lookin' like he was thinkin'.

"Well, now Amandla, I'll bet you your sister wouldn't mind lendin' you that dress she got from your relations on your last vacation South."

It took Aunt 'Mandla a bit to answer back.

"No, I don't think she would mind."

I didn't see her face, 'cause she started to wash the dishes, but Uncle Will was smilin' the rest of the night an' he was still pretty happy the next mornin'.

~~~~~~

When December 31st finally came 'round, Aunt 'Mandla spent the whole day gettin' ready for the party. She'd called my ma at her boyfriend's place an' asked her if she could borrow her dress, an', when Ma told her no problem, Aunt 'Mandla sent me home to bring it back for her.

My house was only like a half a mile away, but with all the slushy snow pushed up offa the street and onto the sidewalks, I'd thought to wrap some garbage bags 'round the dress to keep it from getting' wet. As Aunt 'Mandla was getting' dressed in the bathroom, she yelled to me that that was an' awfully smart thing to do.

Uncle Will was comin' down the stairs in his best church clothes, bringin' down Aunt 'Mandla's jewelry, stuff that she'd got from her visit South.

"What are ya gonna be doin' while we're at the ball?"

I told him I wasn't sure, probably just watch some TV.

Uncle Will kinda whispered to me, "Yer not gonna watch it alone, are ya? Why don't ya bring in one of the bunnies ta watch it with ya?"

Aunt 'Mandla came outta the bathroom lookin' real nice. "I thought that the world was going to end tonight William? Are you sure you still want to go out?"

Uncle Will smiled, "Nah, I think the power might go, but I don't think the world's gonna end. The rabbits are for just in case, ya know."

Aunt 'Mandla smiled.

~~~~~~

I was sleepin' on the couch when I heard 'em come back from the party. I tried to skooch the rabbit offa me 'fore Aunt 'Mandla opened the door, but I was too late, an' I guess it didn't really matter, 'cause Aunt 'Mandla looked happier than I'd ever seen her look before.

They both looked real tired, an' real wet. Aunt 'Mandla said that she was gonna go take off her makeup and went into the bathroom as Uncle Will started to take off his boots at the door. Musta been only a minute or two later when I heard Aunt 'Mandla scream.

She 'bout broke down the bathroom door on her way out, "Will, oh my God, Will! Look at the dress! Look what I've done to my sister's dress!"

A dark orangish splotch was just startin' to dry on the front of the dress.

Uncle will shook his head sadly, "That damn sink. Ya don't think you'll be able ta wash all of the rust outta that, do ya?"

Aunt 'Mandla just looked at me, "I'm so sorry." And she just kind'a plumped down on the sofa next to me.

I was holdin' the bunny real tight, an' he was shakin' real hard under my arm. Uncle Will came over to the sofa and sat down next to us.

"'Mandla, why don't you take that dress off, an' start tryin' ta get as much of the stain out as you can. The power's still on, so I'm guessin' that the cleaner's'll be open tomorrow. We'll take it down an' see what they can do 'bout the stains, then we'll take it to the tailor downtown."

~~~~~~

The next mornin', when they got back from the cleaners, Aunt 'Mandla sat me down on the couch with her. "The man said the dress was taffeta, and he doesn't have the pattern to replace the stained panel." Aunt 'Mandla took a deep breath, "He can remove and replace the stained material, but he'll have to order it, and that will take at least a week or two, and then another couple of weeks to actually put the dress back together. The total cost will be somewhere around $600."

I don't think I was really followin' her 'til she said $600. "Ma doesn't have $600."

"Your mother isn't going to pay for it, your uncle and I are, but your mother expects you to bring the dress back with you when you come home..." Aunt 'Mandla got real quiet, an' softly she asked me: "Would you mind staying with us for a while longer? At least until the dress is finished? I won't be home in the mornings anymore, because I'm going to do some temp. work at the factory with your uncle, but I...I wouldn't mind if you brought in a rabbit to keep you company after school."

Didn't bother me at all an' it sure as hell didn't bother my ma. She was more'n happy to be able to spend some more time with her boyfriend, 'sides, it'd be good for me. My school was just across the way, and Ma thought it'd be good to have someone home with me after school. I kinda felt bad lettin' Ma think that Aunt 'Mandla'd be home with me, 'stead of workin' at the factory with Uncle Will, but I guess I wasn't really *alone*, since the world hadn't ended, I still had the rabbits.

It took a bit longer than four weeks to fix the dress, an' it cost more'n $600, somethin' about the piping an' embroidery, an' there was even more trouble matching the material. But Uncle Will an' Aunt 'Mandla still managed to pay for my ma's dress, an' the plumbin', an', though Aunt 'Mandla had joked about eatin' the rabbits if money got too tight, there was still enough money to feed us.

When I finally went home, an' Ma took the dress outta the bags, I think she looked just about as happy as Aunt 'Mandla did when she came home from the party.

"Wow, your Aunt Amandla even had it dry cleaned for me! I've never seen this dress look nicer. It was so musty and gettin' a little moldy, but look at it now son."

I'm glad my ma was so happy, 'cause Aunt 'Mandla was real tired. Uncle Will'd broken his arm at work, so Aunt 'Mandla had to take a full time job at the factory. An', with the medical expenses an' all, Aunt 'Mandla worked right through the first Saturday of the next November, an' the November after that, an' the next one too. I don't think my ma wanted to go without my aunt 'Mandla. An', 'cause she didn't have no use for it anymore, 'cause she only wore it when she went South, an' we needed the money anyway, Ma sold her dress.

Stuck on "Liquefy"
Blake Schmidt

Hello, guilty conscience and unrelenting skepticism!
Thanks for the bleeding insecurities and tepid wisdom.

It's nice you made it,
Now I'm not so Isolated.

Lately these eyes are jaded.
And in vain I seek the knob
To turn up these lights all faded.
You Shake the hand that I drink with,
And forsake the man that I think with.
Just gimme love or get me numb or gimme something!
You can have this empty prosperity I'm living plump with.
For it's the most fleeting happiness I've ever encountered;
Vapid, Manufactured, and transacted over counters.
My capitalistic tendencies turn my friends into bright green
opportunities:
So we're free to use each other; our Greed and Inhumanity,
mere impunities.

I should've known my inspiration would run away from home
When I left it home alone to go follow the masses.

And I no longer have time to eat or time to find time to be
sober,
Because I'm saving up my sobriety and rations for the day the
robots take over.

And our Timeless Quest for Free Will: soon to be in vain--
When our very own Technology makes us slaves again.

The only thing that's real
And genuine
Is the Pain.
Of not knowing what I might have been, had I been myself.

And not lost my Youth to the disenchantment of my reputation's health.

So once again I have to redefine myself.
This, I know.

But now I'm lost amongst the diversions:

Caught somewhere between primetime TV, downloaded mp3s, a bottle of rum and the softness of her skin;
Caught somewhere between watching Ferris Bueller's Day Off again, channel surfing, filling up my tank and getting too drunk to remember;
Caught somewhere between all my futile attempts to escape Reality, her moistness, getting high, and cleaning up my messes;

My Dreams and Inhibitions,
Emotions and Inner Visions,
Discontentments and Innovations,
Darkest Secrets and Vivid Sensations,

Are all caught in this Blender of Distraction stuck on "liquefy".

Track One

Colleen Farrow

She can lay hours to blame on this emptiness,
confused to heavens,
least to her all stars revealed.
She will spend half a thousand moments too demure,
in pursuit of pity grand or offerings secure.
She can't find the source of selfishness tonight.
In her struggles and her tries for self-empowerment--
a girl half-crazed, infested, without light.
To fall in love, oh they always say: illogical--
even worse to love a man who barely breathes.
Give yourself, give your love, give immediately;
light fires above your reach and watch them burn...
then mourn the distance growing in between.
Digging deeply gouges damage twice--I know it hurts--
you don't have to smile for loss of tears tonight.
Veins and elbows, ribs and bruises,
strange to end the sight...
sick with living, sick with sighing and now this
dying, somehow, lost.
Sweet and tender rains fall from her
as chances catch inside the heart,
make her start and now she's drifting off to dream.
Miles away she wonders if he sleeps,
if love will tame his heart faithfully the same.

A Man Named Poetry

Amanda Goodrich-Stuart

I saw a man today.
He was poetry.
He carried his home
around in a bag
on his back,
swung across his
shoulder.
Cars flashed past him.
He trudged slowly
on;
stopped only once.
Stopped
and stared at the
sign across the
street in front
of the Gables Apartments
as if someone had called
his name
from a window.
"Are you living the way you
dreamed?" the sign asked.
Poetry shifted the weight of
his bag,
momentarily relieving
some weary muscle,
and walked on.

Defenestration

Hall Rd., M 53, Where Ants Still Crawl the Pavement

Andrew Hungerford

1.
The crowd slips along, moving together in thin lines,
like so many wheeled ants
orderly, but for occasions of cross lane swerve

Chemical trails guide, keep the lines moving
from each nest in metallic exodus.
It's easy; not much thought required from
a brain in an exoskeleton
with adjustable lumbar support.

2.
This used to be a small trail
two lane road, bordered by
thick trees, densely packed
like blades of grass.
But years ago they were cut down,
snapped, moved by steel mandibles,
hauled away on strange jointed backs
in a caravan down the road.

Now it is 8 lane divided highway,
hills of dirt line the sides,
cones of soil, pits in the sand
that will soon become
destinations.

3.
"Jackass watch where the hell you're going,
haven't you heard of the goddamn turn signal
ever think about
checking your blind spot?"
"Idiot."

4.
Stopped at the light, cars stretching in carapace black
ahead and behind, I make conversation
with my friend riding shotgun.
"Did you know that ants only leave the nest
when they have just a few weeks to live?"

Mt. Pleasant

John McAuley

The tallest Indian
Is made of concrete and felt.
There is no treaty banning people
From bringing gold to the glass hills
Instead of taking it.
Slot machines are as abundant as the buffalo were
But they can shoot back now.
Geronimo would trade his horse
For a seat here
To laugh inside his vision
That the best scalps are made of green.

Learning How to be Pink
Theresa Mlinarcik

i.
Cloud racing, bubble gummed soles.
Hers were pink
Until she discovered mud.

ii.
Adolescent after-school dances.
Only the pants were allowed to ask.
Packaged in miniskirt wrap
With pink lip gloss bows.

iii.
Ashamed of her bloody ring-finger
But happy to train her breasts with lingerie.
Bus ride "M.A.S.H." sessions to imagine
Dickless Ken Doll husbands
Riding in pink corvettes.

iv.
Sex-smelling and baby-fearing teenagers.
Drinking Diet Coke myths,
Eating magazine models for lunch.
Finally able to bleed
          Pink   anger
For years

Peace Time

Jennifer Heliste

The words spilled recklessly from his tongue
like drops of red wine,
pooling in my ears,
staining my mind.

He told me about his days in the war,
how my black boots
reminded him of his best friend;
the bullet that escaped from the gun
and the bloody stream that flowed from the corner
of his mouth.
He spoke of death as he poured
blood-red liquid between
his own lips.

He told me about his time in Korea
how he once made a man lose his breathe
using only the skin on his palms
and the muscles in his fingers.
He told me how he forced out
the air from his lungs
and the beat from his heart
I shuddered when he put his hand on my arm,
gripping tightly for comfort.

He told me about the skills and the uniforms,
how he was taught to bleed a man
with a government knife,
He learned easily it sinks
into fleshy bellies, cuts
off families, drains life.
He told me how broken the men looked
just before they fell off the blade,
Their expressions like the shattered
glass on our kitchen floor

which leaked
permanent reminders of intoxicated colour.

His eyes were glassy and distant,
    looking into the faces of armed men,
    searching for forgotten answers and impossible
    remedies
Lips dyed crimson from years of drowning in bottled seas,
    his inevitable escape from the stains of his mind.

Safe Sex

Alex Rossman

*(If this poem had been a crayon, its label would've said: To
Be Red Allowed)*

Immaculate ejaculate
Spewed forth,
But no reception.
Doomed to be consumed
By spermicidal contraception.
A miscarriage of messages,
Misconceptions of perception.
Confined in this concubine,
Blessed by Divine interception.
At our midsection intersection,
Separated by Protection.
Cold and clinical,
So close, yet no connection.
Smoke-cloud intentions
And emotions unmentioned,
All in thanks to IntraVenus intervention.
Like breath,
They've been held within,
Engulfed in sin and sensation.
No liability
For these liaisons,
Libido or libation.
No cause or concern
For placebo procreation,
No jumping to conclusions,
Justice or justification.
Simply forlorn fornication,
Cowardly cop out copulation-
No one's exempt
From attempts at temptation.
The womb is softer than the heart to offer
When proffering penetration.

Keep your distance in existence,
Trying to salvage some salvation.
You see,
>Lust is easier than love
>As secretions safely suffocate
>Beneath the latex body glove.
>Keep your intercourse coarse,
>Keep your incidents free of sentiment.
>Hiding behind a hard-on,
>Don't ever let your guard down.
>Stay detached,
>Never get attached
>And they won't ever catch you.
>Keep your armor on under your clothes,
>Never let your self be exposed
>And they can't ever hurt you.

Seventeenth Post

Lindsay Smith

i walked into the room and said to myself "damn it'll be a long night" but the kid at the table brought out his chair from underneath him and swiveled it around as to say "what's up join the club" and i rethought. we shot each other looks and pretended to look lost in thought and all the while secretly knew what each other was trying to do. he was all "i'm higher up not on the food chain but on another chain and hey i'll chain you up" and i was all "psst you think you're the shit but check out my shit don't stank." he schmoozed and flaunted and spread his knowledge and i sat there acting faux stealth and equally faux aloof. but i was on. he was on. he looked at me with eyes that said "baby i'll take care of you till kingdom comes and take out the trash on Sundays with no complaints and all i ask is your love" and i shot back at him "better take care of me and treat me right which occasionally means thinking about me before thinking of you" and i imagined him saying "aight 's deal." and with that we'd elope and glow and own the stars and dominate. but the clock on the computer read 7:58 and i packed up and left early without a word.

To Fly or Fall
Christie Sampson

I stare at you
Over the rim of my cracked coffee mug
You question my thoughts with a tilt of your head
I lick my lips and answer
"Thank you for making me smile."

You helped me to find myself
Made me face my fear of life
Let me believe in you
When I couldn't believe in me.

Hours later
I watch you drive away
Away from me
Away from us
And I wonder how I'll sleep
Waking up tomorrow without you
No one to save me from myself

You always frightened me
The things you made me feel
A thousand ideas, and emotions
Came alive

And I remember
How I changed
When I was with you
Or perhaps
How I didn't have to change at all

"You're letting me go," I had asked
You nodded
And left me with my memories of us
To fly or fall on my own
You said the choice was mine alone

I sit back down and
Trace the crack on the mug
Until it forks

I lift my eyes
And smile

Analog Sigh Through a Digital Pipe
Andrew Hungerford

When six years of
threadbare emotional duffel bags are dropped
carelessly to a sunken concrete front porch
at two in the morning on an
unseasonably warm
October night,
the drying leaves caught in exhale
behind closed panes,
one would hope for more to read than
the whir of a fan,
the click of a keyboard,
the words on the screen,
ones and zeros in pseudo-synapse,
impulses jumping thousands of miles,
while a train's whistle pushes through the outside air,
crossing the personally insurmountable
barrier of wire and cable, sent down the tangled pipes
just to get to the University down the road.
A face would be nice,
Or maybe a breath, let go.
Anything to say that in the morning,
It might all be fine.

Time Cries

Brian Lapp

Circling Inner Images
Mind tying mind
Wrapping illusion shapes
 Of which no-one is aware

 Standing within another time
I long for nothing more
Everything is perfect
When the worse can be ignored
Planting season, sowing time
 Forever onward, never as before

We lost all we strive for
Turning away even as we pray
The moon is merely a reflection
The sun merely a flame
Close your eyes and scream "soleil"
Then I shall be risen

The prism leads to white light
 And the energy of creation
 Brings all within one
From the cave have I striven Plato and the Sun
Enlightened apart from the darkened realm
Far apart from the animal sounds

Journal Entry Made After September 11

Kendra Anspaugh

Flag on the roof of the about-to-be-finished Biophysical
Sciences building on the
      south end of campus.
Flag in the Flash movie Saurabh found on the Internet about
Afghanistan getting
      the shit kicked out of it by our Air Force.
Flag on the Mustang Saurabh stopped to stare at yesterday
and the driver yelled
      at him, "Fucking Arab!"

Engines toward a Personal Renaissance (for Richard Feynman, who was surely joking.)

Andrew Hungerford

Locksmith, bongo drummer,
theoretical physicist,
you were one who knew ars scientifica.

In the twentieth century we became
so specialized,
'I will be a gear,'
'Then I will be a cam shaft,'
that the Renaissance man looked
an obscure painting from before the Revolution,
lost somewhere behind,
paint dry and cracked,
when the automatic wheels started turning.

You saw
when the tumblers fell,
or the photon, positron,
emitted quanta jumped,
it was all about interaction.
Paint in motion,
Pistons in time,
hands to the drum heads,
diagrams on the wall.
Ideas reaching, always moving,
connect and pull,
the engine runs.

After you, QED was no longer Latin,
and existence on its smallest scale became
roiling, turning, rolling,
not a particle in a box, but a foamy machine.

Here I am,
a sprocket with grandiose plans,
grabbing a cam, compressing a spring,
for motion, always motion,
not a mass produced replacement part,
but an original mechanism,
not waiting for the paint to dry
on my revolution.
In the end you wrote that what you could not create
you could not understand.
You, who said,
"I'd hate to die twice.
It's so boring."

Humanity's Closet

Mary Douglas

Stripped naked,
Of excuse, lie, hypocrisy,
Of meaningless platitude,
Unachievable dreams,
Condescending politeness,
What is Humanity?
But a shivering, frightened, homeless,
Piece of flesh crouched under a bypass,
Made by hope, religion and chanced fame.
Hunched over,
Snarling after each morsel,
In attempts to quench a hunger,
That can only be aggravated.
Yet we walk around clothed,
Skin peeking through at Columbine,
In Bosnia, Cheneya, Rwanda.
Ranks of skin-heads supplemented with
Intolerant boy scouts and
Crusading religious fanatics,
Who through devotion know a woman's place.
No, we stand clothed,
Prattling over coffee, giggling about some boy,
Unable to look in the mirror,
At the ugliness, the fat rolls,
The nameless skin devouring disease,
Where are the Renascence nudes?
Austere, prestigious, untouched by gluttony,
As the world whines onward,
I sit,
 Shivering,
Listening to its shouting ignorance,
Knowing my shout of outrage, of horror,
Will be completely ignored,
Knowing I too must walk clothed.

Voided Exposition
Julia Herzog

her nudity surprises him
with her heart tattooed to her elbow
like road kill out on the highway
looking awkward and exposed
flesh bared to the moon's delicacy

rise early in the morning to her screams
harsh breathing slowly dissipates
turning to be shocked by the exposé
of her faltered dreams bleeding from
her lips as she speaks of this pain

dripping around the smooth curves of skin
are the words melting into thought
like your brain laid out in the Texan field
sizzling with the heat of the day
waiting for something to make sense

hold out his sculpted hand and resist
exposure to the surface of temptation
until the revelation can be whispered
as the density of her passions escape
into the stark nudity of day

Night Drive

John McAuley

The windshield is cracked,
Sprawling there like a white spider,
taking tiny nibbles of the wipers
at every pass,
growing larger as rain turns to ice.
It becomes a firm hydraulic jaw,
spreading mass.
It started as a small pebble, very small
on a Rhode Island highway.
It will devour itself
by its own expansion
Until it crumbles at the steel frame
Unless I replace it before Portland.

The Search for John Elliot Sinclair

Laura Portwood-Stacer

(This story is true. I wrote it in January of 2002, however, it takes place in my mind about a year before then.)

College. It all seemed so hip, so cool, so... enriching in my head a year ago. I imagined walking to class under ancient trees, which, by some defiance of nature, shed deliciously golden fall leaves all semester long. And sipping lattes over refined discussions of philosophy in some hidden, but inexplicably ever-bustling, coffee shop. And late-night pizza binges in my dorm full of interesting people with fascinating past lives which they would hide with gumption but then reveal with touching sincerity. Oh yes, and classes taught by illustrious professors with impeccably dry wit to students who would actually appreciate it. And, of course, I would be swept off my feet by some wonderful co-ed with dashing good looks, a sparkling sense of humor, and unparalleled intellect, creativity, and talent.

Um. Well, maybe all that was too much to ask of a campus that shortly before had spawned disgustingly destructive riots over, not social unrest or political protest, but, yes, a basketball game. But I had my dreams, and my faith that there was some subset of the MSU undergraduate population that could fulfill them.

My fantasies were running high the day I came to tour campus in order to make the final call that I would indeed be choosing Michigan State University over the University of Michigan. UofM seemed a much more obvious choice for satisfying my hunger for a worldly and cultivated higher educational experience. But there were other factors to consider, and I had pretty much decided to make the most of what MSU had.

It was a cold February day, but the sidewalks were full of class-bound students, and I could envision the snow melting away to vibrant greens and yellows, and under each parka I saw a potential gem. I wasn't being totally unrealistic though: I had to admit that the classes I had observed earlier in the morning were about as boring as what I was missing in high school that day. And the Shaw cafeteria left a little something to be desired for a picky vegetarian. But I was attempting optimism and doing a darn good job of it.

Last stop on our tour was the Honors College where we talked to all the relevant people and were lastly given a little showing of the building. I don't remember if there is a window in the tiny computer lab downstairs, but there, a palpable "ray of hope" shined in. There were two average sort of guys working together in there, of whom I would probably have taken no notice, except that our tour guide seemed pleased that they were there to serve as an exhibit. It turned out that these guys had started up a literary magazine the year before, and how perfectly coincidental that we should run into them, because I had worked on the literary magazine in high school and felt certain that the staff-members of such publications at MSU were sure to intersect with my ideal "subset." So we chatted with the two guys, who were actually quite funny and engaging (my mother and I later agreed that "the one who was sort of losing his hair was cute" as well). They happened to have a copy of their magazine with them, which they gave to me, and then my parents and I were on our way.

On the car ride home, I began to look through the booklet. Amidst its pages I was bound to discover a brilliant author who would, with words, perfectly encapsulate my college ideal. My hopes were rewarded by a story on page one. Well, maybe "Master of the Universe" wasn't about all the things I wished to incorporate into my college experience, but it definitely gave off a hip-cool-enriching vibe. I could just see myself tracing that route down Grand River, soaking up the delicious circumstance of living on campus among people my age. Maybe it would be me for whom this author, one "John Eliot Sinclair," would be looking, and it would be he, with his clever jokes and adorable social apprehension, who would sweep me off my feet. The magazine fell forgotten on the car seat next to me, and I indulged myself in hazy dreams of my ideal college lifestyle. Yes, I would do all the things I had dreamed of doing in college, and many more, walking arm-in-

arm with the wonderful John Eliot Sinclair (who, for the pur-
poses of my imagination, had begun to take on the appearance of "the cute one" from the Honors College). Yes, MSU it
would be. I would find my "subset" and my John Eliot
Sinclair!

But here I am, sitting in CSE 320, mourning my decided lack of subset and Sinclair. In fact, hardly any of my college fantasies have come true. The fall leaves were here and
gone in a matter of days, and had they lingered, it wouldn't
have mattered because my daily route is traced between Case
Hall, Wells Hall, and the Engineering Building — three of the
most unromantic structures on campus and which have
absolutely no tree-filled meadows within their triangulation.
The latte-sipping is pretty much out of the question because
a) all the coffee shops are about a mile away from my dorm
room; b) philosophical discussion is extremely hard to come
by; and c) the closest thing East Lansing has to hidden-yet-
bustling is "Café Latte" which is unswervingly smoke-filled
and pretentious. The pizza binges would be ridiculous, due to
my realization that all the people who live in my dorm, quite
understandably and forgivably, are just like all the people
with whom I attended high school. In fact, some of them *are*
the people with whom I attended high school, which isn't
their fault, but doesn't exactly lend an air of mystery and
intrigue to their personalities. My philosophy class is indeed
great intellectual fodder, but the professor's impeccably dry
wit (yes, he has one!) is about as understood and appreciated
by the students as a stand-up comedian in an Albanian
monastery. Plus, whatever mental nourishment I might glean
from this class is more than offset by the hours of drudgery
provided by calculus, computer architecture, and algorithm
analysis. And, of course, my knight-in-shining-backpack is
nowhere to be seen. I've joined the staff of the literary magazine, but, while fun at times, even it has proved disappointing.
As it turns out, the staff which promised to be full of "subset"
members does not extend very far beyond the two guys from
the Honors College basement, and even they have left the
country for the semester. Not even "the cute one" can save
me now.

Well. Maybe it's time to reevaluate what "college is supposed to be." Maybe it's not hip or cool. Maybe it's only enriching in that it instills a healthy sense of loathing for the Engineering Building computer labs. Maybe the "subset" is actually equal to the empty set and I'll just have to be content with the people I find. And it's probably true that John Eliot Sinclair is only a pseudonym, and the real author of the story is some geeky boy who is into comic books and Star Trek. Oh well.

I guess maybe these idyllic college experiences don't just happen. If I wanted old trees and grassy expanses, I never should have signed up to live in Case Hall. And come on, if I'm looking for intellectual stimulation and philosophical discussions, the computer science department can only do so much. Yes, some things are out of my hands. But, if "the cute one" leaves the hemisphere, I have to be willing to do a little more looking on campus. So I guess I'll have to continue tweaking my concept of "what college is supposed to be." Maybe move to north campus, change my major, try and track down John Eliot Sinclair. True, he might not be exactly who I expected. He might be a geek. But he might be "the cute one." Or maybe, a little bit of both.

Little Girls in Woman Shells
Lisa Bush

We were sprawled on your bed, remember? The blanket that
you loved was wrapped around our legs and I used your
stuffed bear as a pillow, because I am allergic to down.
Staring at the ceiling: your makeshift collage of cologne ads
and pictures ripped from Cosmo. Ideal lives, or so we
thought. You lit incense and we let it surround us, envelop-
ing. The smell reminded me of concerts in the park, the ones
where the folk musicians played and we were among the few
not smoking away our problems- we tried to blend in with a
crowd that we were only on the cusp of belonging to. It was
dark in your room, except for the candles ... were there candles or did it hurt too much to have any light at all? For once,
I had nothing to say, but I always knew you understood. We
put Bob Dylan on- any other day we would have known that
made us cool, but that night we just needed something comforting. And we thought our problems were so grown-up, but
really who were we kidding? It seemed like the end of the
world to me. Little girls in woman shells ... Magazine pictures
on the ceiling. I swear if it hadn't been for you I would have
died.

Fall
Aryn Bartley

Gina woke up cold the day her grandfather died. There were at least five blankets on the bed, but for some reason she was freezing. Could be the chill of fall seeping in through the window. The leaves were already piling up in long alienated strips along the street.

"Feel this," she said and rolled over in bed to press a white-knuckled hand against Peter's back. He grunted and arched away from her, mumbled something about being late for a train and was silent. Gina sat up and squinted at the clock, glowing an eerie green in the dim light. It was already 7:30 but she was exhausted. They had stayed up late the night before, arguing and then making love before finally drifting off to, in her case, fitful sleep.

Gina swung her legs over the edge of the bed, and picked up her robe, which lay crumpled at the foot of the bed. The floor was warm to touch and she could feel the blood starting to flow again. A good bath should do the trick. Her head felt muddled, cloudy, and her fingers were like ice.

She sat on the toilet, head resting in her hands, while the bath ran. She felt tired. When she looked up again, the bath was full and the tap squeaked a gentle protest as she cranked it to the right. It hurt to test the water, but she dropped her robe and got in. Her feet stung with pain at the feel of the water, but soon she could wriggle her toes and relaxed back against the edge of the tub. The water felt good against her skin.

Lying there surrounded by slow breaths of steam, Gina thought about Peter and the last three weeks. Starting way back at the bookstore, when she first saw him. He was hunched over a book in the philosophy section, his shaggy blond hair curled over the neckline of a ratty black T-shirt. As she passed, clutching a stack of books, their elbows bumped and *One Hundred Years of Solitude* fell off the top of her pile.

"Oops! My mistake-"

"No - it was me, I wasn't paying attention-"

Their eyes met; a smile exchanged; her heart slammed painfully against her sternum. My god, those eyes!
"Are you reading - "
 "Me? Oh - no - it's a present-"
 "Oh for your-?" Eyebrows raised.
 "My grandfather, actually. I've read it though, it's my favorite, one of them, so - I thought- it's his birthday." Had she ever spoken a complete sentence in her life? If this conversation was any indication, no. But he was smiling.
 "It's a good one. When's his birthday?"
 "Almost a month. I'll be going back."
 "Where you from?"
 "Me?"
 "Listen - you want to get coffee or something?"
 They exchanged phone numbers and a slew of pheromones, and later that night, her blood racing with a triple espresso and the most sexual energy she had felt in months if not years, Gina found herself tangled in her sheets with a stranger.
 Three days later he moved in, bringing a stack of Nietzsche, a backpack, and an ashtray. "I don't smoke," Gina said, pointing. "Neither do I, but I used to," he replied. "Actually, I use it to store ideas." Gina raised her eyebrows, trying to suppress a smile. He continued, oblivious. "Scraps of ideas. I scribble them down in those rare moments of inspiration. Which do hit, if you can believe it, once in a while." His bony fingers spread wide, poking the air for emphasis. "I store them in my ashtray, those scraps and at the end of the month I choose the best, the most inspired to pursue. I'm a -" he paused, and laughed self-deprecatingly- "Writer."
 For a moment, the part of Gina that melted with pleasure at these words won out over the instinct to roll her eyes. Another writer. The last time she dated a writer had been devastating. Jaieson, with an I-E. He could only write while drunk, though she personally hadn't noticed much difference. Jaieson's poems had all centered on the lone wolf (male, of course) stalking the "witch" of inspiration. It worked once or twice, but when she found him watering her aloe plant with

Pabst Blue Ribbon, screaming "I'm the wolf, god damn it!
Fuck me, you crazy bitch!" she knew it was over.

But with Peter... maybe there was something there. At
least he could laugh at himself, and she didn't smell any alco-
hol on his breath. Not to mention that he was gorgeous. "A
writer? What do you write?" she asked, running her fingers
down his chest to his belt buckle. "Mostly - umn- ficshuhhhh"
"Fiction?" "Umn- yeahhhh... fiction..umnnnnn..."
And so on, from there.

In the bath, Gina thought about Peter, how quickly
they had become a unit. Already saying "we." We want to see
that movie, don't we? We'll be a little late, don't hold dinner.
Gina didn't know how comfortable she was with it actually.
Her little apartment, which had seemed so clean and pure
before, her haven when the world pressed in on her, was
slowly but surely being infiltrated. A black sock on the bathroom floor. Kant lying on top of her Isabel Allende. Peter's
smell permeating her sheets. She could feel the change in her
body, too. Her lips felt puffy and bruised, her breasts tender,
her bones brittle, like they could be snapped in half by a flick
of the fingers. I'm so tired, she thought. He's keeping me up
too late.

He was inscrutable to her. At the moment, he was
without a job, but he had worked on a daffodil farm near
Sacramento for three months. (Daffodils? Why daffodils? she
had asked. Why not daffodils? had been his rather irritating
response.) He had been a line cook, had worked in the
Alaskan fisheries, had written something, once, that had been
published, though he wouldn't show it to her. It's my past, he
had said, on, on to the future! That's what counts. She had
gleaned that before all this, he had been a home-town boy in
Kansas. I played football, he confided shamefully. But he
never talked about his family. The Monday after he moved in,
she asked about his parents. He turned sullen and stared out
the window in silence. "They don't exist. Expression is what
matters," he said, sitting at the kitchen table in his boxers,
"and Experience. With a capital E." Gina started to smile,
then realized he was serious. Peter had a self-assured, almost
arrogant way of speaking that both attracted and repelled her.

If she didn't get the sense he was utterly genuine about it all, she would be infuriated beyond belief. She waved the keys to the clinic in his face. "I've got to get to work." "Wait!" he shouted and pulled her into his lap for a cold deep kiss tasting of milk.

Gina slumped down in the tub, opening her mouth filling it with warm water. She didn't know how long it would last, this thing they had. She shot the water out from between her teeth. Her space was being invaded. She was neglecting her friends. She hadn't talked to her best friend since she had met Peter. She knew what Maria would say, though. "Ooh, girlfriend! How is he in bed?" And the sex was good, yes, very good. But was it too much? All the great sex in the world couldn't fix the profound differences between them. For god's sake, she thought, he reads old dead white men and wears black. She was so tired.

But soon, soon she would be going home. The stability of home. The smell of a fire in the wood stove, the constant, comforting bickering of her parents. The conversation and the teasing and the gentleness that awaited her in - was it a week? Yes, a week. The knowledge that she could relax and be herself with people who knew her. Playing cards with her grandfather, still strong and smart, the only person she could really trust. No more energy expended in learning about this mysterious, pompous and yet somehow appealing new man.

She thought about the crazy sensuality Peter offered her. Dragged her into. Was it worth it? What did he really offer her? Some conversation, sex. But still. What was really necessary? What did she really need? Was he giving her what she really, truly, needed?

It was too much. Maybe it was time to end it.

Gina pulled up the bath plug and stepped out, dripping. She grabbed her towel and dried her body, then bent over to wrap the towel around her hair like a turban. Using the sleeve of her robe to clear a space in the mirror, she stared at her face. Felt a profound disconnection with the configuration of eyes, nose and mouth staring back at her. The sound of a phone ringing shook her out of her prolonged gaze. Gina stuck out her tongue at her reflection, smiled tightly and turned to the door. Opened it.

Peter was sitting rigid on the bed, phone in hand. "It's for you." "Me?" Something in his eyes, in his sleepy but worried voice made Gina's stomach swoop low into her groin. She stared at his face as she heard Nana's voice come through the line, strangely high-pitched. "Hon - it's Gramps." She didn't hear the rest. Didn't remember hanging up or slumping against Peter. She just sat there on the bed like a dead thing as her new boyfriend smoothed her hair back from her face. She felt his warm hand on her arm. "Get back in bed," he said, pulling back the blankets, "Are you okay? What happened?"

Gina looked at him blankly. "Am I okay?" she said. "I don't really know. I don't really know what I need right now. My grandfather -" Gina took a breath and tried to keep her voice level. Peter wrapped the blankets around her shoulders, drawing her close. "I'll stay with you," he said, "you don't have to say anything." And held her as she cried.

"You're getting wet," Gina finally said, straightening up and pulling her hair back. "Sorry. Can you make coffee or something?" She got up and walked back into the bathroom. The mirror had fogged back up. Gina bent down and picked up a black sock from the floor, then folded it neatly. She heard Peter's voice from the kitchen, "Coffee's ready – nice and hot. Damn, it's cold in here!" She looked down at the black square in her hands. Fall had begun and everything had changed, and she didn't know what the truth was anymore. Outside a single leaf fell from a tree and drifted to the cold ground.

Waiting in Line: Time Spent with Gavin Craig, 1997-2002
Timothy Carmody

I must come clean; I know Gavin Craig very well. At different
times, Gavin has been my friend, collaborator, roommate, editor, classmate, co-conspirator, and confidant. I was there
when he met his wife, and when he married her; at the wed-
ding, I signed as a witness and served as the best man. We
also started a literary magazine together, which became, after
some twists and turns, *The Offbeat*. All of this qualifies me to
refer to him in the first person, and disqualifies me from
being an impartial, dispassionate critic of his work. That's
fine. As Walter Benjamin said, dispassionate criticism is a big
dull pile of crap. (Okay, so I'm paraphrasing.) But part of
what makes Gavin an interesting writer to talk about (and talk
with, for that matter) is that his reading of literature, his work
as an editor, and his reflections as an observer of the literary
scene (both big and small), interconnect with his creative
work in strange, interesting ways. Gavin's *oeuvre* (if any
writer in his early twenties can be said to have an *oeuvre*) has
already extended to virtually every literary genre imaginable:
but each permutation seems to be an uncomfortable one.
Gavin's reinvented himself a half-dozen times, remaining the
quintessential man of letters, but only reluctantly a poet, play-
wright, critic, editor, etc., and so becomes an anti-critic critic,
a poet in conflict with poetry, and so forth. Even his fiction –
the only genre that Gavin has at least ostensibly claimed as
his principal one – exhibits this same self-negating tendency.
Gavin's stories tend to turn into anti-stories, through both
formal disruption and narrative selection – or as his wife
charmingly noted, they very often seem like "boring stories
with no point." Now I don't think this last charge holds as is,
but I repeat it because I think it's hilarious, and all the more
so for hitting on something true.

So I find myself having to refer to Gavin Craig *the man*
as often as I refer to Mr. Craig *the author* (if you please) – if
not more so. And if Kafka's first reviews were penned by his

friend Max Brod, then I don't think my special pleading (if it's seen as that) can negate the quality of what Gavin's done, or what he is capable of doing.

When James Joyce was asked what he thought of Ezra Pound's work, he responded that he hadn't read it, but that Pound was an exceptionally kind man and a good friend. Unfortunately, I have read Gavin's writings, so I don't have the luxury of silence Pound did. On the other hand, I also remember Gavin's response to an editor's introduction to an interview we both once read. After reading aloud a passage that called the interview "a pure pleasure," Gavin wrinkled his nose and declared, "What did he do? Give him a hand job?" So if I'm overindulgent, I know that Gavin will be the first to criticize me. In fact, I know he'll criticize me anyway – and I'm sure it will be hilarious.

Detroit and The Foundations of Irony

When I met Gavin Craig at a semi-formal university function, his hair was long, he wore jeans and a flannel shirt and a baseball cap, and I wore a black T-shirt with an obscene statement scrawled across the front of it. And maybe that tells you all you need to know.

Then again, maybe it doesn't. I liked Gavin from the first. He was loud, with a good laugh, and sense of humor, and we had a common background in the old Detroit suburbs of south Oakland County. There's something highly peculiar about places like Ferndale, Hazel Park, Madison Heights, Warren, Roseville, Center Line – fading, integrated blue-collar communities wedged between the white and wealthy outer suburbs and the black, impoverished city. Not very many kids wind up in drug gangs, but not very many kids go to college either. Gavin and his brother had been raised largely by his mother alone. The two of us had both been childhood exceptions for being smart, and now on top of that, we were exceptions at the university for being poor. So not only did Gavin and I both come out of high school with the same set of references and know some of the same people, we both had the same fears and insecurities, and the same chip on our shoulder. There was a common rebellion against station and location: an attempt to use the university to get out of Detroit (physically and psychologically) while simultaneously rejecting the sterility of campus life. We identified immediately.

Virtue and Purpose

There were also cultural touchstones, of which more appeared as I got to know him better. Reading had been for me something a private affair. My friends certainly didn't read. Gavin read a lot, and talked about books, authors, and movements enthusiastically. To tell the truth, I struggled to keep up. When it came to literature and things literary, he left me in the dust. Gavin had been to Europe; he had read *Ulysses*; he knew the Beats cold. Before I met Gavin I was a mathematician who read the occasional novel for fun. He was the first person my own age who offered and demanded a serious accounting of literature. But what made Gavin different from literature students whom I met later was that he always approached a work with an orientation was pervasively anti-critical. He softened on this opposition later, but he really did think that there were authors and critics, and that theory was strangling the creative lifeline of literature. The purpose of dissecting literature had to be to learn something – about either 1) the art of writing, or 2) the nature of the world all around and the human spirit within – that is, about the art of living. And for Gavin, this distinction – between life and literature – didn't hold much weight.

Which was something else that set Gavin apart from most of the people I knew or had known. Gavin knew what he wanted to do, what he wanted to make his life about. This was to become a writer. But more than that, Gavin was thoroughly convinced that his particular calling, to become an author, was the greatest task a human being could have. Furthermore, he would actively convince you that this was so. I don't think the literature professors at Michigan State encouraged as many young writers as Gavin did, at least as convincingly. As he said in his really quite excellent manifesto "The Required Reading List for the New Revolutionary," the idea of beauty is both *virtue* and *purpose*. Gavin really believed that anyone who had the talent to become an artist and the discipline to devote to the craft had an obligation to try. His commitment made him compelling.

Here and Now

And what he asked for was not always easy to give. He wasn't inter-ested in indulging people, or in taking up the Romantic myth of writing as inviolable self- expression. Gavin had been influenced by the Beats and the post-modern crowd, but he was still something of a Joyce-and-Hemingway modernist. Accordingly, he thought authors had two principal obligations: an obligation to reality and an obligation to literature. He especially deplored the escapism of most student writing, and of popular literature more generally. He didn't espouse a fully-flushed-out realist or naturalist aesthetic, but he insisted that writers examine the *here and now* of their immediate location, including themselves and their relationships and interactions with others, and that they do so unflinchingly. Secondly, he was most interested in writing that extended the craft. He wanted to be a part of an avantgarde literature that would be devoted to innovation and subversion. We both loved the modernist ideal of technique that we saw in *Ulysses, The Waste Land*, and, in its own way, in Hemingway's writing, and Kerouac's: the perfection of a genre through its annihilation. (I could also add here, now, Flaubert, Proust, the Surrealists, Borges, Beckett, and dozens of other modernist writers who tried to pull off the same feat.) This was how to criticize literature – by surpassing it.

Finding A Way Out

Now this was all very serious, but that didn't mean that it wasn't often very funny. If you want to take the line Gavin took, the attitude you have to take up is one I'd call *principled irony*. There's a German word, *Ausweglosigkeit,* "no-way-out-ness," that Bertolt Brecht uses to account for the self-undermining and sometimes despairing tendency in modernism. The Brits might call it (more justly) *taking the piss*. If you combine all three, I think you get a decent feel for Gavin's writing, for its general tropes, for its successes, and where it sometimes seems to go wrong.

After all, there's something inherently funny about the grammar, sentiment, and timing of the line *"Here we write quietly so as not to disturb the livestock"* in "East Lansing Is Not A Good Place For Poetry." But it underscores how Gavin tried to infuse a range of emotions, and a full range of ideas ("The Required Reading List" can be read as an exegesis of this one line alone) into a compact image. So be cautious when Gavin makes jokes – it usually means he is up to something. There's quite a pedigree of this kind of caustic humor, both in the American tradition (Mark Twain, Ralph Ellison, Raymond Carver) and in Europe (Nietzsche, Kierkegaard, and Socrates come to mind) but the figure who comes to mind is Gregory Corso. Gavin read in Corso's poem "Marriage" a hilarious but incisive critique of American culture, an explosion of social norms and their covering mythology coupled with a gesture towards possible alternatives. It's this basic attitude, presented in several different arrangements, that you find in Gavin's oeuvre, whether it's poetry, prose, or drama.

The Genre Problem

Gavin was not especially fond of poetry, although that was primarily the genre he published. He didn't believe he had the gift for lyricism, and his poetry tends to be anti-lyrical. What you get instead is a compression of ideas, combined with a sustained austere persona that is disarmingly constant across his poetry. The address is monological, and personal, but not intimate, almost restrained, while remaining emotionally charged. In the monostich poem "My Father Taught Me To Forget Things," the form really capitalizes on Gavin's strengths while minimizing his weaknesses. The compression into a title and single line avoids lyrical excesses; simultaneously (and paradoxically) it achieves an emotional intensity and proximity exactly by remaining restrained, and distant. It's the brusque vulnerability of a Hemingway story ("For sale: baby shoes. Never used"); it achieves the poetic through the absence of poetry.

The monological impulse in Gavin's poetry developed in two separate directions in Gavin's later work, into nonfiction on one hand and drama on the other. But while these genres were more appropriate to Gavin's talents, their logic didn't really seem appropriate to his ambitions. For all of Gavin's resistance to programs of literary criticism, there's something vaguely deconstructionist about the way he repeatedly negates, cancels, or dismantles the intellectual conventions of genre. But I think this strain runs deeper in Craig's work than the language of deconstruction really suggests the bleakness and emotional tonalities suggest something closer to existential self-destruction, with an eye towards re-invention, than mere postmodern play with form. Also, it doesn't give (at least I don't think) an adequate account of Gavin's frequent blurring of fiction and nonfiction lines as well as those of genre. Gavin places himself, both as author and man, beneath the dissection knife. This points us towards a literature that is not just technical or even psychological but also in some sense moral. There are several aspects of Gavin's biography, along with indications in his own writing, that can provide good reasons why the absorption of literary forms, along with their subsequent annihilation, would be particularly appealing. In addition to those already mentioned, it's important that Gavin was never entirely comfortable in his editorial role in the East Lansing literary community – he was jealous of the time he lost for writing, he was often disappointed by the writing he received and his own work he produced, and was often very upset at the possibility that his creative and editorial work and the work of the authors he nourished might go unrecognized. But what I think Gavin was able to create out of his own biography has been more general.

I think Gavin's writing tries to depict the fundamental gap between our reality and our self-understanding, and the despair that often results from this gap, whether it is recognized or unrecognized. Characters in Craig's work frequently fail to adequately understand one another, and just as often misunderstand themselves, usually because their means of self- or other-understanding, however sophisticated, show themselves to be inadequate. Gavin often said about his writing, especially his fiction, that what he was trying to achieve were resonances, subtle insights into ourselves or others, found in the spaces between characters, bordering on epiphanies in the Joycean sense. He didn't stress as often his love for the absurd, for the failures of the imagination, but it was just as strong. And he found it in idiosyncratic places: probably most notably in Joyce's treatment of *paralysis* in *Dubliners*, and Kerouac's recognition of the failure of the Beat mythos in *Big Sur*. This sensibility makes his writing often difficult to interpret, since just as often even his personae miss the point of importance, or grasp it too late.

Gavin asks as much from his readers as he does from young authors - they must make the connections themselves. ("Only connect!" Forster tells us.) But I think these ideas help us to understand his ambiguous attitude towards genre, and his tendency towards bleak self-defeat. Not only is it the humanist enlargement of the "genre problem," but it does point towards a modern moral resurrection of the basic formula of Greek tragedy - the gap between knowledge and reality, and the inevitable, self-destructive form our actions take when we fail to know.

A Big Fat Asterick

This is not to say that Gavin consistently achieves this effect, or that he does so at a consistently high level of quality. Even his best pieces - I think "The Required Reading List" and "Sketches of Englad" particularly stand out as pieces that mix genres and levels of reality into something new, and positive - don't entirely merit in their *achievement* the lofty characterization I've given here. They do, however, merit it in their *ambition*, which may be a more meaningful level of analysis for a 23-year-old writer. And in ambition Gavin's writing has usually trumped anything set besides it for publication in terms of scope, depth, and maturity.

I have often told Gavin in conversation that I've yet to see his young masterwork - the piece that fully capitalizes his ideas and insights. I'm still waiting.

I think "Sketches of England" points toward what such a work might look like, in its use of modernist montage, its inter-collated use of fictive sources and nonfiction, and in the way it uses these elements to compose itself as a kind of bricolage, a synthesis of elements at hand to meet a particular need. The story uses a multiplicity of representations, reflected and refracted portraits, to try to pull together a dissonant but unified multiperspectival picture that does indeed try to capture something elusive, dynamic. Here Gavin manages to tell you how to read him as you read him, without giving away all of his secrets. But until we see something else, I'm still waiting at the front of the line. I think Gavin's ideas about literature are the right ones, and - I hope - it's only a matter of time before they pay off.

East Lansing Is Not a Good Place for Poetry

Gavin Craig

East Lansing is not a good place for poetry.
There's no place to do it but disinterested coffee bars,
No smoky java joints where you can taste the energy in the
air.
Poetry takes bravado,
And this is no place for such things.
Here we write quietly so as not to disturb the livestock.
Poetry is of the edges,
And we have no edges here,
Mid-Michigan, middle class, a mid-tempo dull existence.
It's far too easy to warm ourselves in complacency,
Muffs over ears, scarves across our mouths,
Eyes half closed against the cold.

The Required Reading List For the New Revolutionary

Gavin Craig

The revolution will not come because those above us are unjust or ready to fall, or because destiny has picked us to lead the way. The revolution will come when we say that it has begun, and act like it has, no matter what the cost. Even then it will not turn out to be what we intended, but it will come.

I. The Change.
"Dulce et Decorum Est," Wilfred Owen.
The Sun Also Rises, Ernest Hemingway.
Look Back in Anger, John Osborne.

Following World War I, there was a cultural and artistic reassessment of morality and values. Perhaps for the first time since the Magna Carta, the divine right of society to dictate the good of its members was questioned. Dadaism declared all of the old moral systems void. Nietzsche was rediscovered. The survivors of a decimated generation looked at their fallen comrades and wondered how any living God could allow such senseless, wholesale, and indiscriminate butchery. Those who had fought, who had been told that what they were going was noble, was glorious, was "sweet and fitting," realized that they had been told a lie.

Eighteen years, one generation later, there was another war, and the good guys won, more or less. America settled into postwar prosperity, a baby boom, and the feeling that the good fight was still being fought, now against our former allies in the Soviet Union. Meanwhile, Europe attempted to rebuild, physically, socially, and individually. Rationing in England continued into the 1950s. Food and basic supplies had to be airlifted into Berlin. World War II pulled the United States out of the Great Depression. Europe didn't quite enjoy the same good fortune.

In 1944, the Montgomery G.I. Bill opened college education to thousands of servicemen. Driven by demand, the
academic marketplace exploded. A college diploma became
an expectation of the middle class, a watered-down status
symbol. Liberal education gave way to job training. As usual,
America lagged behind Europe, but beneath the veneer of "the
nuclear family," something was happening.

Theses:

    1. Modern academia is market-driven, not idea-driven.

    2. The United States, perhaps uniquely, has reversed
economic and cultural roles with its former European coloniz-
ers.

    3. Any American, and particularly any European-
American cultural movement must be fully aware of a living,
symbiotic connection to Europe. Isolationism renders any
movement invalid.

II. Counter-culture and Un-Americanism.
    On the Road, Jack Kerouac.
    The Bell Jar, Sylvia Plath.
    "Marriage," Gregory Corso.

The 1950s are often cited by those who seem to wish
to live in any time except for their own as a halcyon time of
short hair, clean houses, and family values, an almost Edenic
period, unique in human history, when God smiled on his
new chosen people, who had just inherited the earth. Even
though Elvis was about to shake his hips and sexual mores on
the new national television, rebels were still the exception,
and as a rule, they had no causes.

Those who believe that the majority of our problems
would be solved by returning to the working father, stay-at-
home mother, nuclear family ways of the fifties believe an
attractive lie. The American family was indeed nuclear in the
fifties; it lived in constant fear of nuclear annihilation, and
believed, characteristic of the time, that "duck and cover"
would improve the chances of survival should the bombs start
to fall.

Under Joseph McCarthy, America flirted with fascism, and the execution of the Rosenbergs made perfectly clear what the government was willing to do to those it perceived as a threat. Hearings were held on "Un-American" activities, lynchings were social occasions, and the arts fell under increasing scrutiny for "obscenity" and anything hinting at sympathy for socialism or the political left.

In 1956, Lawrence Ferlinghetti published Allen Ginsberg's *Howl and Other Poems*. A year later, and in no small part due to the attention "Howl" was receiving, *On the Road* followed. The Beat Generation became au courant to the stifled and dissatisfied, ironic since, particularly in Kerouac's case, the material had been written close to a decade before. While many of the unconventional and cre-atively-minded found echoes of their own experiences, the work was also finding its way into the hands of an entirely new group of people.

Theses:

4. In the 1950s, America nearly fell prey to the very political movement, fascism, that it had just defeated exter-nally.

5. In calling for a return to the cultural values on the 1950s, the political right is, wittingly or unwittingly, calling for a return to vast social and cultural oppression masked by a delusion of homogeneity.

III. The Second Change - The Baby Boom Comes of Age.

Even though the 1960s are now forty years in the past, it is the opinion of this document that little satisfactory litera-ture has emerged from this period. The noteworthy counter-examples are nearly without exception the literature of histor-ically marginalized ("Un-American") groups—women, homo-sexuals, and Americans of non-European descent. While in many ways, the burgeoning counter-culture of the 1950s can take credit for opening cultural and literary paths to voices which had been previously silenced, it is the very success of the counter-culture, its being co opted by the middle-classes and academia, that led to its own collapse.

As previously described, the Montgomery GI Bill initiated the explosion of the academic market. The maturing of the baby boom, and the relative prosperity of their parents, only solidified the trend. Four years of leisure, exposure to counter-culture literature, dissatisfaction with their own feelings of "adolescent" marginalization, and their status as the most commercially desirable demographic gave rise to a youth counter-culture unlike anything the United States had ever experienced before. For once, the counter-culture had a voice (white, "socially-conscious" youth), a place (campus), and power (disposable income). The social unrest of the late 1960s and early 1970s attests to the counter-culture's strength, and the Civil Rights Movement attests to its desire and ability to do good.

But the seeds of the counter-culture's demise lay, perhaps, in its own nature. A counter culture has strength and focus only so long as it has a force to oppose. As the baby boomers grew in social, economic, and political strength, as they entered the workforce and the market catered more and more to their (as opposed to their parents') demands, what had been the counter-culture became simply the dominant culture. "Hippies" became "yuppies," and the social consciousness of the 1960's became the materialism of the 1970's and 1980's, a materialism that was all the more secure because it was rooted in social consciousness.

Now culture promotes many of the same marginalizations that it once fought against, and even believes that those who still cry injustice are simply unaware that their complaints are obsolete. There are still calls to return to "simpler values," and those who once rebelled try desperately to believe that they indeed, everyone else, were happier in the past. There are even those who would return to the use of divine mandate to silence opposition.

Theses:
(See thesis #1)
6. The co-opting of the counter-culture by the middle and particularly the upper-middle class in the 1960's led ulti-

mately to its demise. Materialism and the market over-
whelmed social concern and the individual. There was simply
too much to lose.

IV.   Our Alternatives
        Letters to a Young Poet, Ranier Maria Rilke
        A Portrait of the Artist as a Young Man, James Joyce
        The Zoo Story, Edward Albee
        "A Supermarket in California," Allen Ginsberg

Here the format changes. Here the document ceases
to describe the past. Who we are is only part of who we can
become. Here, statement of thesis will precede description,
and here the numbering starts over.

1. *On some things it is better to be silent than to speak
poorly.* This is both a key postulate and an apology for omis-
sions this document has made. "Required" is not "comprehensive." This thesis also precludes imposition. One may not
speak for another.

2. *Beauty is both virtue and purpose, and is both stat-
ic—a quality or state of being—and dynamic—an action of
transitory state of becoming.* Beauty, here, is a broad term,
and the key forces opposed are those which interfere with the
ability to create, discover, and become aware of beauty, both
externally (fascism), and internally (self-deception). Beauty,
emphatically, is not mere physical appearance. It is transitory, and easy to miss. We have to learn how to look.

There is a corollary to this thesis. There is no absolute
method to beauty. Beauty is not a scientific proposition,
although scientific propositions can be beautiful. Self-sacrifice, however, is one of the more reliable paths, in no small
part because true self-sacrifice is nearly impossible. (Sacrifice
in order to obtain a greater good is, in many ways, not true
sacrifice.) Exercise in paradox and contradiction is instruc-
tive.

3. *The pursuit of beauty is creative.* In this usage,
"creative" is social and cultural as well as purely artistic.

Here the theses end. Systemization has its limits.
From here we can only be descriptive. To do otherwise is to
betray too far too many of our virtues: improvisation, accura-
cy, and individuality. While the pursuit of beauty can never
be other than solitary, we can outline the common cause. To
here, things described have not been of our making. To here
the stories told have been of those who came before. To here,
the choices have not been ours. Here, this changes. Here we
begin to make our own rules, and our own mistakes.

There is the work we do, the work that has always
been done, and there is our work, the deeper, secret work. To
be American is to be displaced, either to be descended from
those who gave up what they were to come here, or from
those who were here and had it taken away. We are not who
we were, and have no desire to be. Our task is the creation of
place, our place. America's birth pangs have lasted three cen-
turies. It falls to us to be the midwives of our own delivery.
This is the revolution, the creation of place.

V.

I will tell you what I will do and what I will not do. I
will not serve that in which I no longer believe whether it call
itself my home, my fatherland, or my church: and I will try to
express myself in some mode of life or art as freely as I can
and as wholly as I can, using for my defense the only arms I
allow myself to use—silence, exile, and cunning.
. . . I do not fear to be alone or to be spurned for
another or to leave whatever I have to leave. And I am not
afraid to make a mistake, even a great mistake, a lifelong mistake, and perhaps as long as eternity too.
—James Joyce
*A Portrait of the
Artist as a Young Man*

To love is good, too: love being difficult. For one
human being to love another: that is perhaps the most difficult of all our tasks, the last test and proof, the work for which
all other work is but preparation.

—Ranier Maria Rilke
Letters to a Young Poet

19. Accept loss forever.
20. Believe in the holy contour of life.
—Jack Kerouac
*Belief & Technique for
Modern Prose, List of Essentials.*

54. Organize your own army and advance on
Washington.
—Tuli Kupferberg
1001 Ways to Beat the Draft

My Father Taught Me To Forget Things
Gavin Craig

Birthdays, and the distances between us in moments together.

Walk-in
Gavin Craig

Characters
      Erick, a student
      Andrew, his roommate

Setting
A dorm room, the present.

ERICK *is sitting in a chair with his back to the audience. There are a number of dirty magazines spread out on the bed in front of him.*

ERICK: What's that Miss Klum? You'd like to introduce me to your friend Tyra Banks? Well, there just aren't enough swim-suits to go around. I guess you'll have to share. . .

ANDREW *comes in through the unlocked door, causing ERICK to quickly zip up and try to close all of the magazines.*

ANDREW: Don't bother going to the caf. Dinner's awful. (He notices ERICK's activity.) What are you doing?

ERICK: Nothing.

ANDREW: Nothing? You were at it again, weren't you?

ERICK: What?

ANDREW: You were jacking off again!

ERICK: Dude, calm down.

ANDREW: (Picks up one of the magazines) Every time I leave the room! I can't come back just once without having to watch you put yourself back together?

ANDREW *drops the magazine on* ERICK's *desk, and* ERICK *chases after it protectively.*

ERICK: Well, if you would give me a little more time...

ANDREW: (Winces) I don't even want to hear it.

ERICK: C'mon. Like you never flog the bishop.

ANDREW: Not like this! This is the second time I've caught you today!

ERICK: It's my exercise routine. You do sit-ups, I spank the monkey.

ANDREW: That's disgusting.

ERICK: Whatever. Sit-ups, cold showers, you do it however you want. My way is more fun.

ANDREW: At least you could do it on your own bed.

ERICK: I don't whack off on your bed. What kind of a sicko do you think I am?

ANDREW: I saw you!

ERICK: You saw nothing.

ANDREW: You were right there! In front of my bed!

ERICK: *In front* of your bed. It's not my fault you took the bottom bunk.

ANDREW: (Picks up magazines) No more. Or these go out with the trash right now.

ERICK: Aw, c'mon!

ANDREW: I'll do it! You know I hate these things.

ERICK: I paid for those! Half of them you can't even get around here!

ANDREW (Reads the cover of one of the magazines) "Fabulous Fakes: Faces you know, asses you don't."

ERICK: All right, all right! I'll lock the door!

ANDREW: You'll what?

ERICK: I don't know, but I'll do something. It won't happen again.

ANDREW: Promise?

ERICK: Or may my balls fall off. Now gimme those! (Takes magazines back from ANDREW.)

ANDREW: Now, if I catch you again. . .

ERICK: Yeah, yeah, I know. I'm going to the bathroom. I'll be back in an hour.

ERICK *exits, magazines clasped firmly to his chest.*

Who's Gonna Ride Your Wild Horses?
Gavin Craig

Characters
    Sam, a guy
    Max, his friend
    Jess, a girl

Setting
Outside a bookstore. MAX is reading a paperback novel. Sam is engrossed in a pornographic magazine.

MAX: What a surprise. Another crappy John Grisham book about a crappy lawyer. The guy really needs to explore some new territory.

SAM: (Unfolds centerfold) Now here's something worth exploring.

MAX: Wow.

SAM: Bet Grisham never wrote about anything like that.

MAX: Yeah. How in the world do they get the Rottweiler to. . .

SAM: I don't know, man, I don't know.

MAX: Speaking of Rottweilers, isn't your girlfriend supposed to be meeting us?

JESS: (Enters) Sorry I'm late.

SAM: Speak of the devil.

JESS: What's this about the devil? (Sees the centerfold) Oh, now that's disgusting! (She tosses the magazine to the ground.)

SAM: Aw, c'mon.

JESS: I leave you alone for one afternoon, and this is what happens? I can't believe you still associate with this filth.

SAM: Christ, here we go again.

MAX *picks up the magazine and starts to flip through it.*

JESS: Watch your mouth! Blasphemy is worse than lust!

MAX: Remind me again how you two started dating?

JESS: And you! You lead him astray!

SAM: Geez, Jess, it's just a magazine.

MAX: "Just a magazine," nothing. This is "Farmland Fornication," the best shit there is.

JESS: (Grabs magazine) Excrement is exactly what it is! And the worst kind! Relations with animals!

SAM: (To MAX) I told you not to buy the one with the animals.

MAX: (Grabs magazine back from JESS) She's your ball and chain, why should I suffer?

JESS: Ball and chain!

SAM: All right, Jess, let's just go.

JESS: I won't have you spending time with this heathen. He'll lead you astray!

MAX: (To himself, but audibly) Wait a minute. . .

MAX *begins to consider* JESS, *and then the magazine, each in turn, as* JESS *continues.*

JESS: Just like those magazines lead people astray, and not just men, but the girls too! They take something beautiful like animals and the countryside, and they make it dirty!

MAX: But the horses and. . .

JESS: And even horses! Beautiful, majestic horses. . .

MAX: It's you!

SAM: What?

MAX: (Show SAM the magazine) It's her! In the picture, it's really her!

SAM *looks at the magazine, and at* JESS. *They hold eye contact for a beat. Finally,* SAM *and* MAX *look at each other and burst into laughter.*

JESS: He'll lead you astray!

JESS *storms off.*

MAX: Dude, how long have you been dating?

SAM: Three weeks. It's pretty serious.

MAX: I'll say.

Piece of Cake

Lisa Bush

When I was little I used to love the swings. I'd kick my feet really hard and close my eyes and it felt like flying. Way up there nobody could touch you.

After awhile I knew the drive so well it was simple to get there and back. No problem, piece of cake. I put myself on auto pilot and pretended it wasn't so hard. I turned the radio up and sang at the top of my lungs, screeching. That was one benefit to having the car, I guess- I could sing at the top of my lungs and no one could hear me, stop me.

It was across the street from a gas station. An ordinary gas station. Mobil or something. You never think they put things like that in front of ordinary, everyday, things-you-see-all-your-life gas stations. Seems out of place. Not very fitting.

Walking in there was the worst part. It must have been worse for him, walking in there every day, having to stay. Should I be mad at myself for hating it so much when I know it was worse for him? Is that selfish? How I am I supposed to feel? These are the questions no one knows how to answer.

So I get a pat on the head. No problem, piece of cake. Drive there, drive back. Just an errand. Like getting the groceries, picking up the dry cleaning.

I would walk in and know there was some weird shit going on in the place. I felt like I didn't belong, or at least like I really badly never wanted to belong. Sometimes a doctor would come out with him and give me some kind of cryptic message to pass on to the family. Tell your parents he moved to level two.

My face must have given it away.

It's a good thing, it means he's making strides.

Strides?

This is the breakthrough we were waiting for ... Just tell your parents, ok? Tell them he moved to level two.

Hard to tell, not very much emotion. He looked the same to me.

There's a kid staring at me, his eyes pouring right through me. He could have been thinking anything ... it was a weird place. I'm not your sister, kid.

I just want to get out. Apparently, a lot of people come here. (End up here?) That's what they say anyway. Can't tell me who, it breaks confidentiality. Besides, I don't really want to know. Some don't leave, though, that's a fact.

We would get in the car together and I'd turn the radio back on, wondering if the station is ok with him. It's like having an elaborate glass sculpture as my cargo. I don't want to go to fast because then I might break it. What would break him now? How am I qualified for this responsibility?

He would always have a paper bag with him, the kind you put your groceries in. How ironic. The contents varied from day to day. Soy milk, packets of peanut butter, wheat crackers. Carefully calculated caloric energy, a specially designed diet of things I consider condiments. A challenge for him.

So level two, huh? Nice work.

I would never know what to say. How do you congratulate someone like that?

I didn't even know what it meant. Did he eat? The thought baffled my mind, it was really out there. Did he talk about It? It that caused all this? I never knew I could hate someone I didn't know.

On one hand, just hearing that there was "strides" made want to stop the car, get him out, and run around in circles, celebrating. Level two! I didn't even know what it meant but it had to be better than what we had so far.

At the same time, he was my glass. I didn't want to inadvertently break him.

Just tell your parents, ok? (No problem, piece of cake.

Some nights I would stay with him so my parents could leave the house. I'm not really sure what they did, I don't even know how they could leave, although I understand wanting to. Even coming here, it makes me feel guilty sometimes. Is it right for me to leave like that? I feel like I'm giving up sometimes.

They would ask me, do you mind staying? It's ok if you don't want to, but we need to make sure someone is here, and we think it should be family. We're family, you know.

We're family, you know.

I would stay there with him. I'd stay in my room, on the phone, or just sitting. It wasn't really difficult- piece of cake, right? No, I can't go out, I have to stay here. Just because ... my brother's sick. Yeah. Yeah maybe some other time. Have fun.

It's not like I was babysitting- he was too old for that. I was just there, so he'd know someone else was there. If he were alone it might be too much. Something could happen. Glass, remember?

Offbeat
William Branch

When I saw a monkey jerking off on my remote control, I knew it was time for me to leave.

About six months ago, my roommate Tim announced that he was going to buy a pet monkey. I simply nodded my head in hazy compliance. Between the completely troubling legality of the whole situation and what I presumed to be troublesome task of obtaining the afore mentioned primate, I assumed that this would be another one of Tim's narcotic induced schemes. Needless to say, I never again need to be reminded of what they say about assumption being the mother of all fuck ups.

The day could have easily been categorized with all the other nondescript days that I have filed away into the dusty cabinets of my long-term memory. So many of these cabinets have gone unmaintained for so long that I think they have been thrown out by the slothful janitor who is preoccupied with indulging in the works of Salinger to the sounds of Satchmo, or maybe he just enjoys a long drink too much. I wish it were one of those days. I returned home from a long day of lecturing and the constant struggle to stay conscious, and all I wanted to do was bury myself in the welcoming cushions of my couch. I was half way there, with the small of my back starting to submerge in tattered upholstery, when I heard a maddening laugh drawing ever closer to my door. The sounds of Dr. Martins pounding against cheap carpeting drew ever near.

Tim burst through the door with the smile of a demon across his lips. His arms were wrapped tightly around a medium size pet carrying case. He bounded over to me and exclaimed with child like delight, "Tom man, you gotta check this out."

His hand flew to remove the latch that restrained the caged door. I stared at the chrome grating in exhausted expectance, but nothing happened. The seconds rolled by in hushed anticipation. As I waited, visions of kitties and puppies danced my head. I started to picture a tiny black and brown mix puppy running around the apartment. It would be the type of puppy that I could fit into my coat pocket until he got bigger. Then I would pass the days playing Frisbee with him. I would toss that disk into the horizon and he would return back to me with slobbering joy and gratitude. If only my friends were that loyal. At the end of the day, he would curl up at my side and I would spend the night running my hand over his fur. I bet he would like Count Basie. I could almost feel a warm tongue licking my face, then the caged door burst open and my fantasy exploded in a mass of high-pitched squawking and unevolved fur.

The thing leaped out right onto my chest. I stared into its dark eyes that were offset against its white furry face, and it stared right back at me. Its tiny black body froze for a second as we gazed into each other's souls. I do not know what he saw at that time, but I can now say that, in that moment, I stared into the heart of evil. Then it lifted its head, and in a flurry of arms and tail, it emitted another high pitch call and leapt into the back of the foreign jungle.

I decided to let Tim keep the spider money based on three principles. First, I believed that this little bundle of joy could be domesticated. Second, I thought Tim might slip up and kill the damn thing. Third, Tim paid half the rent.

Tim had taught it some novel tricks in six months, but one of the more amusing of which was teaching the monkey to smoke. Through dedication and persistence Tim taught the guy to take drags of cigarettes. He had him up to half a Marlboro light a day, and he was halfway to achieving my second principle.

When Tim was around, the monkey was a model roommate. He stayed near Tim and was rather loyal and quiet. The second Tim left it became a whole new predicament. The thing would jump all over the furniture clawing and chewing the whole way. Tim dismissed these damages as growing pains. I wanted to jump on Tim and start clawing and squawking. Then we could see how he felt about growing pains.

One day, I returned home from class before Tim, and

it happened, the sight that would lead me to where I am now. I have had a lot of time to think about this and I still do not know if he was doing it out of pure hormonal lust or vindiction for me. I strolled into the living room, and there on top of my coffee table, was my remote control upon which that monkey sat as it gyrated and jerked until it brought itself to a peek that any 15 year-old boy would have been jealous of. The monkey just looked up at me and smiled.

I had already gathered my bags together and thrown them into the trunk of my car by the time Tim returned. I filled him in on the whole traumatizing ordeal, and I reassured him that I would be back in a few weeks. He asked if there was anything he could do to make me stay, and tried to comfort me with the knowledge that he would try to train the monkey better. I just looked at him straight in the eye and said with earnest conviction, "Tim, how am I supposed to watch TV?"

Author Biographies

Richard Lund is a chemistry major of Michigan State who will be graduating this spring if he's lucky. His hobbies seem endless, as you might find Richard skateboarding, publishing zines, weight lifting, giving tattoos, or even the occasional lap dance. Besides the current task of graduating, Richard hopes to soon finish filming and editing his second skate video "Almost Evil: 665" which is the sequel to "Suck The Cool Right Out" which was released at the beginning of 2002.

Colleen Farrow is a sophomore at Michigan State University and an English Major who, like most other English Majors, loves to read and write. She writes mostly fiction and creative non-fiction; her favorite author is (and will forever be) J.D. Salinger. Her other obsessive loves include coffee, running, asparagus and the MSU library.

D. Harlan Wilson's fiction has appeared in a number of American, British and Australian magazines, among them Identity Theory, Redsine, Samsara Quarterly, The Café Irreal, The Dream Zone, Fables, Locus Novus, Thunder Sandwich, Minima, Wildclown Chronicle and 3 A.M. Magazine. He has published two books, The Kafka Effekt and 4 Ellipses, and his third book, Stranger on the Loose, will be out soon. Currently Wilson teaches composition and literature at Michigan State University. D. Harlan Wilson's official website is www.msu.edu/~dhw/dharlanwilson/enter.html.

Greg Wright, a Ph.D. candidate in English at Michigan State University, enjoys watching movies, reading books, writing, and many other activities that involving sitting down. Sometimes, he likes to spread outlandish lies about himself just for fun. He is the smartest man alive.

John Garcia is an employee of Michigan State University's College of Osteopathic Medicine. When he is not dealing with facts and figures, he enjoys cooking, reading and contemplating the nature of the universe. He is currently working on putting together his first book, which he hopes will do very well.

Chris Bigelow will be graduating this spring in English secondary education. His love of the natural world and his family's beef cattle farm provide him with many of his musings. These most often take the disguise of poems but an occasional short story slips out every once and awhile.

Submissions

The Offbeat encourages contributions by all individuals, student or not, Michigander or not, American or not. Our only criterion is quality.

All submissions should include a cover letter with the author's name, address, phone number, and e-mail address. Electronic submissions can be sent as Microsoft Word or plain text documents to offbeat@msu.edu . Printed submissions should be sent in a 9 1/2"x11" manila envelope to:

The Offbeat
Submissions Editor
1405 S. Harrison, Ste. 25
Michigan State University
East Lansing, MI 48823-5202

There are no minimum or maximum length requirements. There are also no limitations on content or language. If your printed submission is accepted you must be able to provide an electronic version.

Submission Guidelines

The Offbeat accepts any sort of literature or art, including but not necessarily limited to: poetry, fiction, drama, creative non-fiction, literary criticism, visual narrative, or any combination. There are no minimum or maximum length requirements. There are no limitations on content, language, or number of submissions. All submissions are roughly divided into poetry, fiction, and non-fiction and are reviewed anonymously by our genre boards. Please do not put any identifying information on the submission itself, but do include a cover letter with your name and contact information.

Check *The Offbeat* website for deadlines.
http://www.msu.edu/~offbeat

About the Offbeat

The *Offbeat* is an independent literary collection series devoted to publishing a diverse collection of voices, and to promoting contact and discussion among Michigan writers. It is run entirely by Michigan State University undergraduate students, and is centered in East Lansing. Student editors encourage contributions by all individuals with a Michigan connection, past and present, visitor and resident, urban and rural, student and non-student alike. The *Offbeat* presents and explores creative works in fiction, poetry, drama, essay, criticism, image, and that which defies categorization. The purpose of the series is to call attention to voices both emerging and established, including those that have been previously overlooked.

Editor:	Theresa Mlinarcik
Design Editor:	Julia Herzog
Fiction Editor:	Bailey Follette
Poetry Editor:	Jason Swantek
Fiction Board:	Jennifer Jennings
	Amanda Goodrich-Stuart
Copy Editors:	Bailey Follette
	Amanda Goodrich-Stuart
Advisor:	Julie Loehr

http://www.msu.edu/~offbeat

Printed in the United States
132009LV00001B/88/A

9 780870 136788